THE URBAN DILEMMA

Christians can reject those people who make up the city by building homes, churches, and fellowships in the safer suburbs.

They can give up on the city, even though they remain in it, by building walls of apathy, resignation, and self-centeredness . . .

OR THEY CAN ACCEPT THE CHALLENGE OF THE CITY—TO STAY, TO PARTICIPATE, TO LEARN, TO GROW, AND TO SHARE.

METRO-MINISTRY is a resource book to help church leaders deal with the urban dilemma.

Metro-Ministry

Edited by
David Frenchak
and
Sharrel Keyes

David C. Cook Publishing Co.
ELGIN, ILLINOIS—WESTON, ONTARIO

METRO-MINISTRY

Published by David C. Cook Publishing Co., Elgin, IL 60120
Printed in the United States of America

Library of Congress Catalog Number: 78-72935
ISBN: 0-89191-101-4

CONTENTS

Preface   7
PART ONE
    THE URBAN CHALLENGE   11
 1 A Biblical Theology for Urban Ministry   12
 2 The Sociological Nature of the Urban Church   26
 3 Urban Church/Urban Poor   43
 4 Developing Black Leadership in White
    Denominations   51
 5 Church Growth in Black Congregations   58
 6 Toward an Urban Church Strategy   65
PART TWO
    THE CHURCH FACES PROBLEMS   77
 7 Churches in Changing Communities   78
 8 Antidotes to Victim-blaming   92
 9 Churches and Energy Conservation   101
10 Urban Fatigue   115
PART THREE
    THE CHURCH THAT MINISTERS   125
11 The Ministering Church   126
12 Viability of Alternate Urban Life-styles   135
13 Radical Ethics   148
14 The Gifted Urban Lay Person   153
15 The Urban Church Revitalization Process   164
16 Ministry among the Urban Indian   174
17 Urban Church Evangelism in a Multiethnic
    Society   188
PART FOUR
    RESOURCES   195
18 Strategies for Urban Reconstruction   196
19 Consultation for Assistance in Developing
    Urban Ministry   205
20 Ministry Resources in Community Systems   212

PREFACE

Although there is a critical need for the church to
bring its resources to the urban environment, there are
indications that the church has chosen not to invest
itself in the city. Following an initial demonstration of
concern in the late 60s and early 70s, organized Christianity seems to have drawn back and focused its attention elsewhere. The city therefore remains an enigma
and perhaps an indictment to the institutional church.

But an ethnically-mixed society is only as healthy as
its level of respect for and responsiveness to its minority
components. Such a society cannot exist with justice if
systems are unconsciously designed or consciously

manipulated to benefit the dominant group at the expense of another. This is true of the church as well as every other social system. If the church is going to grow and flourish in the city, it must resolve the question of its role in a heterogeneous environment.

Still, there have been a few churches and individuals who have chosen to demonstrate the viability of the gospel in the urban context. These churches and people represent a variety of institutional, historical, and methodological perspectives. The theological glue that holds such a montage together consists chiefly of two ingredients: a devotion to the person of Christ and a corresponding desire to be involved in building the Kingdom of God.

Metro-Ministry is a collection of addresses given in May of 1978 at a Congress on the Urban Church. The Congress was sponsored by the Seminary Consortium for Urban Pastoral Education. This collection (as the Congress itself) is designed to reflect a variety of experiences and perspectives and to bring about further understanding of the nature of the city and the urban ministry.

It is hoped that the reader of this book might be left with three impressions: a new understanding of urban ministry; the realization that although there is a desperate need, there is indeed hope for our cities; and the conviction that urban mission is one of God's priorities in today's world. If the church fails here, if we deliberately ignore the city and its pressures, there is no gospel that we can preach with integrity anywhere else.

Appreciation is in order to the six seminaries that have made a conscious decision to allocate resources to the training and education of urban pastors. They include Associate Mennonite Biblical Seminary, Bethel Theological Seminary, Calvin Theological Seminary,

North Park Theological Seminary, Northern Baptist Theological Seminary, and Trinity Evangelical Divinity School. A special work of thanks to the David C. Cook Publishing Company for making this material available.

David J. Frenchak
Director
Seminary Consortium for Urban
Pastoral Education

PART ONE
The Urban Challenge

One

A BIBLICAL THEOLOGY
FOR URBAN MINISTRY

Raymond Bakke

SEVERAL YEARS AGO, a well-known Chicago minister asked me to recruit a youth director for his large, historically liberal congregation. Said he, "I've got to admit you evangelicals really know how to run youth programs."

He was right, of course, in his observation; programming has been the specialty of conservative Christians. In recent years, franchise organizations and syndicated seminars have been proliferating around the nation about as rapidly as McDonald's hamburger establishments. We are disseminating programmed theological messages and methods tailored by computers, consortiums, and consultants according to the latest data from

Raymond J. Bakke

  Dr. Bakke is the pastor of Fairview Avenue Baptist Church in Chicago. Dr. Bakke's church is in a Spanish neighborhood, and the congregation is a heterogeneous mix of seven ethnic groups.

church-related market research. In keeping with this trend, few ministers or missionaries would attempt to manage ministries without goal-oriented programs and clearly defined objectives. Media ministries abound, and the very best resource persons in technology are in constant demand.

Person-centered or relational theology is a second and equally popular motif in evangelicalism today. Even though some groups have turned to person-centered theology out of frustration with the shortcomings in more structured programs, this movement is bringing renewal to many churches. The search for community by an increasingly alienated and mobile society has provided opportunity for churches to function as extended families. Churches of many different traditions are discovering again both the New Testament emphasis on the house-to-house nature of the Christian faith and the contagion of our incarnational gospel's application. Ministry models, both within and without local church structures, are functioning in cities. Many of these contemporary urban ministries appear to be more self-conscious and less prone to cultural captivity than some of their historic rural counterparts.

The idea that evangelicals will covenant among themselves to live out their Christian commitments in the most desperate of urban neighborhoods has biblical and historical precedent. Although in a few cases their theology of persons founders in subjectivism (or naivete), other manifestations of this movement have brought new hope to some of our cities.

But have we solved our problem? Have our sophisticated programming and our incarnational models fulfilled our mission in the city? Not entirely. By itself, Christian planning technology has not kept churches in the city anymore than the same technology has kept banks, supermarkets, or good schools in the city. The recently announced abdications of a major food chain and numerous insurance companies from downtown Chicago were dictated by the same assumptions that prompted the departure of many churches and church-related institutions.

It is my conviction that at least part of our weakness is due to an inadequate understanding of our biblical resources. Broadly speaking, urban churches have resources in at least four categories—biblical, historical, geographical (or environmental), and congregational. A dozen years of study, ministry, and observation in Chicago has led me to conclude that while each of these ought to contribute to the shape of our urban ministry, our biblical resources are the least understood and applied of the four.

A TALE OF FOUR CITIES

When the Swiss Anabaptist George Blaurock faced expulsion from Zurich in the Reformation Era, he told civic officials he would rather die than leave the city. He cited Psalm 24:1, "The earth is the Lord's," as the basis for his preference. Beyond sheer courage, Blaurock espoused the theology of place—a biblical mandate for urban concern. Without that kind of theology, the church may never reach the urbanized world with the gospel of Jesus Christ.

Some people have charged that conservative Christians have failed to function in the cities because they take their Bibles too literally. The Bible's milieu is essentially rural, say these observers. God makes gardens; evil men make cities. David, the king of Israel, was a nice country boy—a man after God's own heart—until he moved into the city and got messed up in politics. In this kind of perspective, Jesus Christ is remembered more for his wilderness camping experiences than for addressing the urban multitudes.

Such an argument ignores the fourteen hundred references to cities in both testaments. Let us study the following tale of four cities: Sodom, Nineveh, Babylon, and Jerusalem. We admit at the outset that there are enough data in the records, biblical and otherwise, to prejudice us against all cities everywhere. But that is only part of the story.

From Sodom, we learn about Abraham's godly motive in his prayer of negotiation to save the city (Gen. 18). Ten people could have saved it from destruction, for God was on record as not wanting to destroy the city. He did so finally for the want of godly persons on the streets. Notice also that God provided for an urban witness in Sodom and was able to distinguish the one, Lot, from the many on the street. That motif—the one in the many—is common in both testaments: Rahab the harlot picked out from among all Jericho; the woman with the hemorrhage in Mark 5 whose touch claimed the Lord's attention despite the crowd.

The Sodom story also shows us that an escape theology was not enough to guide the people God allowed to flee the city. The sorry sequel of Lot's life, sketched at the end of Genesis 19, reminds us that to flee a city does not give Christian individuals or institutions a new morality. Who can say, after all, how much ecclesiastical incest and ego-tripping has followed in the wake of exurban church relocation to safer places? Let us also not forget in our hurried glance at Sodom that of all her sins, the one God hated most and the one for which she was ultimately destroyed was, according the the prophetic commentary of Ezekiel 16:49, her failure to take care of the poor and underprivileged in her midst.

Nineveh was one of three ancient Assyrian capitals. Like the twentieth-century Nazis, the Assyrians ruled over a terrorized captive empire. Their evil was the very reason they needed the gospel. At a time when prophets such as Jonah and other patriots in Jerusalem saw the world in terms of "us against them," God revealed his own plans for that foreign city. The story of God's concern for Nineveh must be studied with the context of God's call to the prophets Jonah and Nahum.

Jonah resisted the mission at first, but, by the grace of God, both the messenger and the message reached that city eventually. No permanent program was established; no persons were identified by name. The focus of the story is the city as a whole, and the massive repentance that ensued was reported to have included the king. Later, the prophet Nahum condemned bloody Nineveh. Apparently the revival had run its course. Among the lessons from Nineveh are these: God is the Lord of all cities; our message is universal; and God is willing to forgive everyone, including the enemies of his people, even when his prophets can't or won't forgive them.

The results of Jonah's evangelism might have been conserved by creative follow-up, or institutional ministries, or national reconciliation with Israel—but none of those things happened. Hence the revival dissipated, and the God who is slow to anger, and who gave a century of opportunity, became furious at their rejection of him. God takes no pleasure in the death of the wicked, said Ezekiel, and that is probably why some people and some cities lived so long.

God keeps his promises. Nineveh was destroyed and was not even found again until archaeologists stumbled over the ruins in 1847 while following the trail of Alexander the Great.

Babylon, like Assyria, was a cursed invader who took massive populations into captivity. This city is the Bible's paradigm of *the* evil city. Even as Judas betrayed Christ, so Babylon, a kind of corporate Judas, destroyed God's city Jerusalem and the Temple and terminated the monarchy. Babylon, in fact, was so evil it could serve as a code name for Rome in the New Testament. But by the grace of God, Babylon was given the services of some of Judah's choicest leaders, including Daniel and Ezekiel. Babylon became the place in which God tutored his people in many subjects to prepare them for their return to the land, and even for their later dispersions in New Testament times to other lands. Certainly the intertestamental theology is much richer because of the Babylonian experience. Babylon received the witness of God by word and miracle, God's grace triumphed in that city, and the gospel penetrated both palace life-styles and government decrees.

Jerusalem, God's city of peace, witnessed some thousand years of ministry throughout both Testaments. In fact, one can observe in the historical books alone at least two dozen different kinds of urban ministries performed largely in Jerusalem. A city on a hill, Jerusalem was to serve as God's visible legacy to the world. Its institutions as well as its individuals were given worldwide responsibilities. Jesus, too, loved this city and wept over it in prayer. The Gospels, which show us God's visible heartbeat, show Jesus weeping twice—once at the death of his friend Lazarus and once at the impending death of his city Jerusalem. This same city demanded and witnessed his execution.

What do we learn from these records? Among other things we can see that to whom much is given, much is required. In Jeremiah's lament over Jerusalem, God reveals that this city's destruction is greater than that of Sodom, because her privileges and responsibilities were greater. Lamentations 4 is one such passage of grieving. (This lesson has ominous implications for my city, Chicago, which has received an incredible share of the church's resources in its brief 145-year history.)

When we study Jerusalem, we also learn some remarkable ways in which heaven is said to be modeled after it. Like it or not, we have an urban future! I have found about 119 cities listed in Scripture. Of course there are differences between the metropolises of the ancient world and the modern city-states of the West. But there are also some similarities we can extrapolate and learn from. Ezekiel 16 shows that cities are mothers of towns, and that there is a sense of wholeness about the environment. There are creative mandates as well as redemptive mandates. There are many urban themes in the Kingdom theology.

FOUR CAREERS

We can also learn from biblical persons and their ministries. Let us consider briefly the careers of four: Joseph, Daniel, Nehemiah, and Paul.

Some thirteen chapters of sacred text are given to the career of Joseph, an economist whose two seven-year economic plans mobilized the entire resources of Egypt to fight famine. Working with a pagan pharaoh, this godly government official plotted a strategy for budget surpluses as well as deficits. He bought land, the text says, by decree; he moved people into cities and fed them by means of direct government action to the apparent benefit of many people, godly and ungodly alike. Not a single pejorative word is spoken of Joseph's economic ministry in either testament. While neither condoning or condemning his conduct in office, we can observe that indeed there is precedent for committed Christians whom God calls to wise and just rule in times of national emergency, even in corrupt political systems.

Daniel is another political model—a young lad who apparently refused to believe that his God was dead just because the Jewish Temple lay in ruins. Daniel learned how to distinguish between his faith and his culture, his convictions and his opinions. And if ever there were a task for Christian education in the city, it is to sort those things out. Daniel became God's instrument in a pagan palace and grew into someone who, as a wise counselor, made the apparently harsh policies and practices of the Babylonian government much more just. He also made use of government institutions and individuals. By doing what God permitted and, in fact, required of him, Daniel taught us that it is possible to minister within corrupt government institutions, be they located in Babylon, Washington, or any other city. Again, no criticism comes of his more than half a century of public service. Is it even possible (and this is purely speculation on my part) that the Magi who sought the newborn Christ (Matt. 2) came because of the oral or written witness of Daniel and its historical tradition?

Nehemiah, a government official in Persia, took leaves of absence to help rebuild the captive city Jerusalem. Among other strategies, he appears to have used the principle of the tithe; he recruited at least 10 percent of the populations of towns and suburbs to move back into Jerusalem to rejoin the clergy who were already there in order to rebuild God's model city. Such service was considered worthy of commendation and prayer support, according to Nehemiah 11.

Paul of Tarsus was, as every early-church historian knows, a thoroughly metropolitan man whose ministry followed the contours of the urbanized Roman Empire. Whether he went first to these cities because the Jews and synagogues were there, or because of a conscious urban strategy, or even personal preference, is probably debatable (and among church historians and New Testament scholars, it is being debated).

Nevertheless, though he was himself an itinerant evangelist, he varied his methods, messages, and emphasis from place to place and was careful always to leave the church in the city in the hands of a very diverse and gifted residential leadership. The early church was urban long before monarchial bishops imposed external organization on it. Commitment to urban places was accompanied by the development of resource persons and organized programs.

The early church did not develop an external hierarchy and support system until the third and fourth centuries. The best scholarship I have found suggests that it did not do so because the environment demanded it, but because the presence of heresy demanded it; that is, Kenneth Strand, A. D. Nock, Adolph Harnack, and many others have shown that in the Roman Empire political power was flowing from west to east, but the ideas and heresies were flowing from east to west. The gospel also went from east to west. As Gnosticism challenged the church in the second and third centuries and rocked it to its foundation, the church was forced to define itself on what historians call the three C's—canon, creed, and church organization. The point is that long before the early church had a monarchial bishop, an episcopacy, an external support system, or anything that approaches the kinds of systems, denominations, and structures we have today, it was able to function in hostile urban environments. And when the structure came, it did not come because the city or the environment required it, but because apparently the attack of heresy required strong leadership at the lay level. Episcopacy principles then began to take hold in the third and fourth centuries.

E. A. Judge, a Cambridge scholar, suggested that most of the early Christians, but by no means all, were artisans, freedmen, and slaves. Philo, who sometimes can be believed, suggests that 40 percent of Alexandria in Egypt was Jewish, and that they lived in poverty and worked in industry. It was to those kinds of urban ghettos that the early church moved. The office of deacon and other offices in the church evolved through the congregation's attempt to care for people in the urban setting.

CHRISTIAN PRINCIPLES

The late archbishop William Temple referred to Christianity as the most materialistic of all religions. Indeed it is. The Bible begins with the work of an active Creator who makes and enjoys his world. It concludes with the world's remaking at his eschatological intervention. Between its covers, the Bible shows how God redeems people in times and places while centering on the incarnation and resurrection of real bodies—Christ's and ours. Christianity is the only religion to integrate so holistically the spiritual and material worlds, both individually and corporately. In our Bible, people willingly identify with their cities. Those same cities are held accountable for their people and policies as public trusts from the Lord.

White middle-class evangelicals seem to have fractured this biblical holism until we have been stripped of a vast, legitimate spiritual power. We have strained out the geographical gnats, as it were, by our exodus to the suburbs, but we have swallowed urban technology like so many proverbial camels. As Christians, we celebrate the fact that we have few geographical meccas, at least officially, but have we not gone the other extreme? Granted, church and mission organizations may be wasting millions on buildings and equipment in a foolish display of rampaging materialism; is that reason enough to deny the validity of the material altogether and to withdraw from corporate or institutional witness in urban communities? For many, if not most of us, it has not taken a Rapture to remove our churches from our major cities. When will we learn that the blessed hope of the church is the Lord's intervention and not the church's migration?

Furthermore, the early church rejected docetic christology. *Dosete* is the Latin word for "to seem"—Christ just seemed to have a body; it was vaporish, ghostly. The church affirmed Christ's real and physical body. Should we likewise not reject docetic ecclesiology and affirm that Christ's church body is also real and institutional?

And if the answer is yes, let us begin to grapple with the signification implication of our confession. Where urban community issues involve property and institutions, the church ought to seek property and minister as an institution in that place with integrity and intentionality (and, I might add, without apology). In the name of the incarnate Christ who became flesh and dwelt among us, we must stop thinking that cities will be reached with impersonal happenings and media crusades. Biblical Kingdom doctrines and corporate solidarity motifs should likewise deliver us from the tendency to exclusivism, individualism, and all attempts to limit ministry to a single frequency or a cultural homogenity. We must take urban places seriously; moreover, we must take biblical theology in its wholeness and allow it to shape our mission mandates.

Urban, cultural, and linguistic pluralism, along with institutionalized evil, will not yield to prepackaged formula witness and simplified answers. The "evangelical blitz" is not enough. In my city of Chicago, McCormick Place has become a kind of Christian clubhouse-on-the-lake where Billy Graham, Bill Gothard, and other kinds of Christian groups hold equivalents to Woodstock; the saints come out, enjoy each other, and use the city as a kind of amplifier to reach to other places, much like the Chicago seven did. They found that the media is in the cities, and therefore groups come to the cities not to reach the cities directly, but to use the cities as means to other ends.

Evangelistic rallies in amphitheatres and stadiums run the risk of merely using the live crowd as a stage prop in order to communicate to people who are invisible—those who are watching in an impersonal way. The dangers, I think, are obvious. It's not that these media campaigns are valueless but that in the name of an incarnate Christ we seem to be more and more preoccupied with such an approach.

We fought a war in Vietnam like that. We parked our planes on Guam, an American base, flew in squadrons of American-built B-52's with air-conditioned cockpits to bomb people to hell from thirty seven thousand feet, and then flew back for a night's sleep. While we were pulling out ground troops, we increased the bombing—and lost the country. Our technology said we should do it that way: it is safer; you don't shed as much of your own blood. But everybody knew that to pacify a Vietnamese village or hamlet, one had to be present there for maybe a thousand years. Americans were not willing to pay that kind of price, so we substituted our impersonal technology for the conventional form of warfare.

I see Christians doing that in an attempt to reach cities; we retreat to technology in the name of reaching the masses, failing to realize that the masses in fact are so diverse that one must proliferate the frequencies in order to reach them all.

I got a call one day from a North Shore woman who was trying to get Chicago churches to transport people out to a Hinsdale or Deerfield theater somewhere to see the film *The Hiding Place*. Ironically, it was one of the few Christian films with an ethnic, urban theme. So I said, "It strikes me as very ironic that you're asking the whole city to be bussed to the suburban theaters to see it."

"You sound like an interesting person," she replied.

Five minutes later the distributor was on the phone long-distance to ask, "What's the problem?"

"I want to know," I said, "what kind of a decision-making process suggested that you should market this film totally outside cities."

He said market research had shown that they do not reach cities with films. And then he added, "Besides, we've gone with the mass marketing coupon system in which the rights for distribution were syndicated. So the organization has committed itself to showing a film for never less than two dollars anywhere in the nation."

Most of the neighborhood theaters in the cities charge less than that. Thus, by a management decision, the possibility of using a film with some ethnic appeal, had been chopped off in the name of technology and mass

24

marketing. And to me, the idea of bussing a city to a suburb to see the movie is even more absurd. The city of Chicago has more people than thirty of the fifty states, and taking them out of the city to be converted is like asking fish to jump in a barrel so they can get caught.

In my community, 49 percent of the people do not have telephones; fifty-three of the eighty-eight churches are in languages other than English; and that doesn't include the storefronts. The cultural heterogeneity is so great that one must think small rather than big if one is going to reach the big city. That is the nature of cities. It was Seneca (the Art Buchwald of his day) who said, "All roads lead to Rome, and all sewers also."

My section of the city includes fifteen different kinds of population groups with very diverse needs, and that does not include all the linguistically different people. What we need is diversity, intentionality, and incarnational styles instead of impersonal media blitzes.

CONCLUSION

We dare not remove our Christian congregations from our cities. Rather, let us propel them into corporate witness, risk, and even urban confrontation when necessary. Our gospel, which by its very nature is good news and not good advice, should deliver us from all forms of urban paternalism, imperialism, and racism. Can we not see ourselves as redeemed members of the one fallen human race and willingly identify with an increasing number of displaced and migrating persons who are coming to major cities all over the world? If Christ has made us free, then we are free indeed—free to minister in the city without excuse, apologies, or fear.

Two

THE SOCIOLOGICAL NATURE OF THE URBAN CHURCH

Anthony Campolo

ONE OF THE MOST IMPORTANT facts about the urban church of the 1970s is that it, to a large degree, ends up serving poor people. We are all aware that in the last several decades, the wealthy have tended to move to the suburbs, leaving the socially disinherited behind. Therefore, the urban minister must understand the kind of religion that poor people find appropriate if he is to be effective in the inner city.

Ernest Troeltsch, one of the greatest students of the sociology of religion, points out the particular kind of religion that appeals to the poor. He calls it sectarian religion, and he distinguishes between the *sect* of the poor and the *ecclesia* of the middle class.

Anthony J. Campolo

Dr. Campolo is chairman of the Sociology Department at Eastern College, where he has taught since 1965. He previously was on the faculty of the University of Pennsylvania.

SPONTANEITY VS. STRUCTURE

The first distinction between the two is that sectarian churches tend to have worship services marked by spontaneity and high levels of emotion. The ecclesiastical churches, on the other hand, tend to be more formal and rational in presenting their message.

When I go to a middle-class church, I often feel I'm attending a religious lecture rather than really participating in worship. Ecclesiastical worship tends to be a performance conducted by the minister and the choir, and the growth of the church depends on how well they perform. The congregation is merely a group of spectators. In the sectarian church, God is the spectator, the congregation performs, and the clergy and choir are simply prompters.

I belong to a black church in West Philadelphia—not because I'm a great social reformer, but because our community changed and black folk moved in while white folk moved out. Our family never left the church, primarily because my father had donated the offering plates! One just doesn't walk out and leave one's offering plates with a bunch of blacks he doesn't even know. So we stayed.

Eventually I became an associate pastor in this now-black church. It's an incredible experience to preach there. What you do, if you want to preach a good sermon, is not to impart some great theological insight, but to recite an eternal, biblical truth to which people can respond with *amen*. In my church, if everything else fails, and you feel like you're not communicating at all, you just stop in the middle of the sermon and shout, "Isn't Jesus wonderful!" That will bail you out immediately.

The sectarian church tends to be a religious pep rally

in which everybody gets together to give God a tremendous hurrah.

Middle-class religion is entirely different. After a good middle-class sermon, people exit saying, "I got a lot out of that this morning." But when you come out of my church, the best thing you can say is, "Didn't we have a good time with Jesus today?"

Of the two, I honestly believe that middle-class Christianity is the deviant form. Instead of the suburbanite trying to bring his Christianity to the city, it is about time we realized that the Christianity closest to the New Testament already exists in many storefront churches.

Uppity people from the suburbs have a lot to learn from inner-city sectarian churches. The average middle-class worship service has a schedule beginning at eleven and ending at noon. If it's not over promptly by twelve, people start squirming and coughing. If the Holy Spirit wanted to move in that kind of church, he would have to clear it with three committees at least. And then they might give him some time during the announcements. Everything else is already tightly structured—even the prayers are written.

In my church, you never know what's going to happen. Even on dead days—the pastor will be a third of the way through the sermon when he'll stop and say, "It's not here. You know what I mean? The Spirit isn't here. Now we're not going on with this service until we begin to feel the presence of the Holy Spirit." And people will come to the altar, and we'll pray until we get into it at last.

The church has not left the inner city—only the white Anglo-Saxon Protestant church has left. And perhaps that was not really Christianity anyway; so good riddance. What remains in the city storefronts is a vital, biblical Christianity, not middle class, WASP religion.

EDUCATION VS. EDIFICATION

The second difference between the sect and the ecclesia is that the sect has no hierarchy of leadership. Middle-class churches are concerned with hiring "educated people" (whatever that means) who have been seminary trained to lead the church.

In many of those little storefront churches, we find people who, in the words of Billy Sunday, "may know as much about theology as a jackrabbit knows about Ping-Pong." But somehow they seem to have captured the essence of the gospel—if not in a rational, theological form, at least in a poetic form that raises the emotions to a love for Jesus that is not found in most ecclesia structures.

The church has thrived best when it wasn't so concerned with a professional appearance. Why did the Baptists and Methodists dominate the early American frontier while Presbyterians and Episcopalians did not? Part of the reason was because the Presbyterians and Episcopalians demanded that only seminary-trained, ordained people be allowed to preach. And the frontier was developing faster than the seminaries' capacity to fill newly created pulpits. The frontier churches were little groups of ten, twenty, or thirty people who needed a pastor who could support himself by plowing fields or tending a store during the week and then preach the "simple" gospel on Sunday. Thus, while the more formal churches looked for educated professionals, the Baptists and Methodists were sending out people who felt "the call of God."

Strangely enough, however, organizations that start as sect groups have a tendency, over a period of time, to become transformed into the very kind of ecclesia structures against which they originally reacted.

The Wesleyan movement, for instance, was a sectarian rebellion against the overly formal Church of England. But it ended up being rationalized and structured into an ecclesiastical institution similar to the one it originally rebelled against.

Sectarian movements are alive and spontaneous; but often when they succeed, they tend to become formal, structured, and rational. They begin to look for ordained, professional specialists instead of people who are filled with the Spirit.

Now if I have a choice between a Ph.D. who knows Hebrew or someone who is filled with God's Spirit, my choice is a simple one. Hungry sheep don't want some Greek verb parsed; they want the living Word.

My own church is fairly large. When our pastor died and we started looking for a new one, some people like myself said we ought to get somebody who was sophisticated and well trained. In the end we did get a man who was highly educated, graduating from one of the top seminaries in the country. But the congregation wasn't awed by that—what they wanted to know was whether his preaching reflected the fire of the Spirit radiating through him.

Which direction would Jesus have gone? When he started his movement, did he recruit the top scholars from the University of Jerusalem? Did he insist on scholarly expositors who thought they knew how to be *relevant*? Or did he pick some fishermen who smelled bad, a couple of exprostitutes, and a midget named Zacchaeus? Face it—Jesus had a zoo on his hands. If you don't think so, look at James and John—a couple of urban losers. They were the kind who would have walked up and down Clark Street in leather robes with *Sons of Thunder* painted across the back. They might have ridden around on camels with racing stripes.

The fact is, these people were not sophisticates. If Jesus had wanted people with credentials, he would have chosen the Pharisees. Instead, he took the people society said were nothing. It seems startling to me that in the face of this our middle-class mindset has opted for pharisaical values, the values that eventually nailed Christ on the cross. When Jesus chose leaders for his church, he was more concerned about their potential to be surrendered to the Spirit than he was about their former training or background.

SALVATION VS. SOCIALIZATION

In sectarian religions, membership is based on conversion, not on socialization. Middle-class churches are filled with second-, third-, and fourth-generation Christians who have been raised in the church. We have to admit that there's a difference between Christians who grow up in the church and those who come in from the outside as converts.

In many of our churches, we have lost the capacity to even understand conversion. William James, in his book *Varieties of Religious Experience,* made it clear that when he went to look for genuine conversions, he could not find them in mainline, middle-class churches. He had to go to sectarian, inner-city groups.

Some of our churches would be embarrassed if somebody came down the aisle crying at the end of a service—they wouldn't know how to handle the emotionalism.

Far-reaching changes in personality resulting from dramatic conversions have become rare events in most established churches. Thus, I find it the ultimate in arrogance when those of us who rarely experience genuine conversion say, "You know, they don't have real Christianity in the city anymore."

CONVICTIONS VS. CONCEPTS

Sect groups are much more exclusivistic than ecclesia groups. That is, the more middle-class one becomes, the less inclined he is to say there's only one way. Dogmatism is offensive to comfortable, middle-class thinking.

I boarded a plane out of Los Angeles one night—a "red-eye special"—at 11 P.M. I planned to get some sleep because I had to teach a class the next morning at eight. But, of course, the guy next to me wanted to talk.

Now I have two ways of handling such people. If I feel like talking and they ask me what I do, I say, "I'm a sociologist." Then they say, "Oh, how interesting. There's a lot of things I'd like to ask you."

But if I really want to turn somebody off when they ask what I do, I say, "I'm a Baptist evangelist." That usually shuts them up.

But when I told this guy I was an evangelist, he said, "Well, I want to tell you what I believe. I believe that going to heaven is like going to Philadelphia.

"There are many ways of going to Philadelphia—by plane, by train, by car, by motorcycle, by hitchhiking. The important thing is that we're all going to the same place in the end."

As we came into Philadelphia, the airport was fogged in and the wind was blowing. The engines of the 707 bobbed up and down in the gale. Everybody was silent. And I couldn't resist. I turned to my seatmate and said,

"I'm sure glad the pilot does not subscribe to your theology."

"What do you mean?"

"There's some guy in the control tower," I said, "who is sending out messages something like this: 'You are four degrees off beam . . . a little more to the right . . . that's it . . . forty-two degrees by northwest . . . you've got it, now stay on the beam, don't deviate.' I'm sure glad the pilot's not saying, 'Aw, c'mon. There are many ways into the airport.' "

There comes a time when broadmindedness is not a virtue. There are times, in fact, when to be narrow and single-minded is the greatest virtue that one can possess. The gospel is that Jesus is the way, the truth, and the life, and no one can come to the Father except through him. In sectarian religion, the inner-city lower class knows how to proclaim that message in a way that suburban whites can't imagine as they try to get along with everybody.

CHRIST VS. CULTURE

Sectarian religion has a strong tendency to reject the dominant culture. Middle-class churches tend to embrace it.

In America today, that means that true Christianity is for losers. That's why Jesus said that not many rich, powerful, or prominent people in this world will become his disciples.

Frankly, I get tired of the brand of Christianity in middle-class circles that tries to communicate that Christianity is for winners. I'm tired of seeing evangelists parade Miss Americas before their audi-

ences to say, "I want to tell you what Jesus did for me."
I'm tired of the church presenting star athletes who say,
"Jesus is my Savior," as though if I walked with Jesus,
I'd be a star, too.

I ran the 100-yard dash for my high-school track team,
but I wasn't very good. In the city championship, our
coach pulled our best runner out of the 100-yard dash
and put me in his place. He knew we couldn't win the
100-yard dash because Bartrum High was running a
young man who would later win an Olympic gold
medal. So coach took his worst 100-yard dash man (me)
and put me against this great athlete, and then inserted
our best runner in the 440-yard relay. He figured he
might be able to win the latter even if he had no one who
could win the 100.

So I was up against the best runner in the state. Fortu-
nately, he was a friend of mine, and he loved Jesus and
belonged to the same Bible club where I had been converted. The third entrant in the 100-yard dash was
Frank, who was also a Christian in our Bible study
group. Since the three of us had practiced and run together all season long, we knew who always finished
first, second, and third. And barring the intervention of
the Lord—namely a heart attack or a bolt of lightning,
both of which I was praying for—I was doomed to third
place.

On your mark, get set, go! And we were off down the
straightaway. And I finished third, which was last. It
sounds better to say third, doesn't it?

The press surrounded the winner after the race and
asked him to make a statement. He said, "I want to thank
Jesus. It was Jesus who enabled me to win."

Frank turned to me and said, "Hey, Tony, what's the
Lord got against us?"

I've got news for all the champions of the world. Jesus

identified not with winners, but with losers. It was no accident that he was born to the enslaved and beaten Israelites who were under the heels of powerful Italians. (Honest, it's in the book!)

In the struggle between the "haves" and the "have-nots," Jesus does not remain neutral. And we who are affluent and powerful must realize that when Jesus takes sides, he doesn't side with us. The only way we can get close to Jesus is to somehow empty ourselves and, like Jesus, take on the form of servants.

The reason sectarian churches reject the dominant culture is primarily because the dominant culture has rejected them. Those of us who have been accepted by the world, who have been made rich by the world, are the ones who love the world. In the black church, the happiest songs are about dying. The sad songs are about living, struggling, and suffering. Chariots swinging low and carrying people to heaven are eagerly awaited. Middle-class people have a harder time grappling with the gospel because they aren't so eager for a trumpet to sound, calling them to leave this world and all that's in it.

Only those who are oppressed and beaten find it good news that this world is not their home. To them, it's good news that the status symbols of this society mean nothing, and that wealth is in fact an encumbrance to true spirituality. It's hard for the affluent and powerful middle-class to affirm those truths with much passion.

THE ISSUES

If the white suburban churches don't have a superior form of Christianity, what can they offer inner-city people? What problems can suburbanites help with? There are several. And surprisingly, since political power is wielded in suburban citadels, suburban Christians are in a better position to effect some inner-city changes than their urban counterparts.

The first problem is that of *redlining*. Certain banks watch the city carefully to see when an area begins to change its racial structure. When black people begin to move in, the bankers look at the map and, as the name indicates, draw a red line around that section of the city. That means they will no longer lend money for mortgages to people who want to buy property in that area.

The impact of that decision is awesome. Let's say you have a house in the redlined area that you need to sell. If buyers can't get mortgages, you can't sell your house. There's only one thing to do—drop the price. But even if you drop the price ten thousand dollars, you still can't find anybody who has that much cash. At that point, the slum landlord comes in with a hundred thousand dollars and buys ten houses at the reduced prices. And then he rents out the houses for exorbitantly high monthly rates. (The welfare system allows people money for rent, but not to buy.) At three hundred dollars a month, it's not long before the landlord has recouped his entire investment and is making enormous profits. And there's no point in maintaining the houses, because if they deteriorate sufficiently, they'll be condemned, and the whole thing can be written off as a tax deduction.

As I watch my city deteriorate under the impact of redlining, I hear some white folks saying, "When *they* moved in, *they* tore the neighborhood to pieces. It's really run down since *they* started living there." Friends, the problem doesn't lie with *them* who are renting there. It lies, as Ephesians 6:12 says, with principalities and powers and world rulers of the present darkness. It is those powers against whom we must wrestle.

A second economic issue is *the tax structure*. In Philadelphia, the school system has failed to open in September, while the city spent its money providing services for people who live in the suburbs. This is true of most cities. Who pays to make the art museum go? The city taxpayers. But who goes to the art museum? Suburbanites. Philadelphia built a new stadium for forty million dollars. We couldn't open our schools, but we built a stadium on a bond that was floated. But if you look around the stadium whenever the Eagles or the Phillies play, you'll find that most of the people are from the suburbs—the poor from the city can't afford tickets. The Philadelphia airport was a fifty-million-dollar reconstruction job. Who flies those jumbo jets? Not the blacks from North Philadelphia, but they're paying for it nevertheless.

We have two names for welfare, don't we? When white suburbanites are on the receiving end, it's called "public service." God is not mocked.

And then there's *low-cost housing*. No one can live in a project unless their income is less than eight thousand dollars a year. That's fine. Poor people move in. Then we send in social workers to help these people—give them a vision, train them, help them get jobs. And we succeed. But when someone succeeds in becoming self-sufficient, he usually ends up making over eight thousand dollars a year. Immediately he must move out of the low-cost housing area.

What must it be like to grow up in a community with no adult models of success? No wonder many are calling low-cost housing a conspiracy against the poor. Any community would degenerate under those conditions.

Yet suburbanites continue to ride by and say, "Look at that. Three years ago it was new, and look what they've done to it." It has nothing to do with race; it has to do with economic structure.

Suburban political power controls most of these matters. Yet why should a suburban legislator oppose redlining? His constituents are unaffected. So nothing is done. It's about time we had a whole new breed of political leaders who don't look simply to the next election, but to the next generation.

WAYS OF MINISTERING

There have to be new ways of ministering. The socially disinherited have never had the problems that middle-class Christians have had with reconciling social action and evangelism. That's a white problem. It was never a problem for black churches. The black preacher preached the gospel on one day and manned the picket line the next, and didn't see any problem with functioning on both levels.

Latin American Christians don't even know what *social gospel* means. All they know is that Jesus came to deliver them, and that means the soul is free from sin, the body is fed, the naked are clothed, and the poor hear good news.

This should be the task of our churches, too. One of the ways this can be done in our cities is through self-help projects. People can be trained to make salable products—macrame pocketbooks or plant hangers, for instance—and then put to work. The church can provide marketing outlets for these products.

Another way of ministering is to buy stock in some

influential corporations. Some of my friends and I have just bought stock in one of the largest banking establishments in Philadelphia. Why? Because we don't like redlining, and we're going to be at the next stockholders' meeting to introduce policy statements that will abolish the practice. Will we get away with it? Of course, because we're going to make sure the press is there, and we're going to ask for a show of hands. And I'd hate to be a white man voting for redlining in front of a TV camera.

We must also learn the power of economic boycott. Years ago in a ministerial meeting, Leon Sullivan pulled out a newspaper and showed us that Tasty Cake, a big baking company in the area, needed thirty new drivers. So a committee was sent to talk to them and was told that the company didn't want black drivers. This was some years ago, and at that time the company claimed it would create tension.

Leon said, "Well, if Tasty Cake won't hire black people, then black people won't eat Tasty Cake." Sales dropped by 27,000 cakes in one day! The company changed its policies.

What does all of this have to do with the gospel? Well, Satan operates on two levels. (And if you don't believe in Satan, then you haven't walked around the city very much. I can see why some people wouldn't believe in God, but I can't see anyone not believing in Satan.)

The first way Satan operates is through the flesh. He moves into the basic drives of our personalities and perverts them for his purposes. Satan can and does destroy God's prophets through misused sex, gluttony, and the will for power. We don't often talk about that last one—the temptation to become number one. Some of us in our pastorates are more concerned in making a name for ourselves than spreading the Kingdom of God.

We want to work in the inner city not because we have a passion for the suffering people there, but because we know we'll be seen as being relevant.

We have to examine our motivations very carefully before we get involved in urban ministry. We need a recommitment to the will of God, a recommitment to let God's work increase while we decrease.

The second way Satan operates in the world is through the principalities, powers, and rulers of this age. One of the greatest insights of our time came from the Mennonite theologian Berkhof, who said the principalities and powers are the political and economic institutions that oppress us. They are clearly seen in the inner city.

Principalities and powers were created by God, according to Romans 13. But just because God creates something doesn't mean he controls it. The best evidence of that is you—you were created by God, but he doesn't necessarily control you. Likewise, principalities and powers were created by God, but some have come under demonic influence.

Look at advertising, for instance. The United States is a country in which people who have money already have everything they need. Yet the economy will collapse unless these people continue to buy vast amounts of consumer goods each year. How do you get people who have everything they need to spend their money on things they don't need? By getting them to believe that certain items will gratify their deepest spiritual and psychological needs.

"Buy a Dodge—it'll give you a whole new image." What's for sale here? A new car or a new image? And then we don't understand why some poor black in downtown Philadelphia, who's been on welfare, who's the last to be hired, first to be fired, who feels like next to nothing, will take his welfare check and buy a Dodge. Then we condemn him for buying something extravagant when we ought to be attacking the principalities and powers that convince him a car can give him the dignity he needs as desperately as work, food, and shelter.

I could go on. "Canada Dry tastes like love." Can you imagine that? Or this one: we know that blacks and whites are alienated—the Africans, the Dutch, the Rhodesians, the Russians, the Chinese are all tense and bickering. But we've received the good news—without Pentecost, it happens on a hill—black and white, orientals and Africans—all holding hands and singing together, "I'd like to teach the world to sing in perfect harmony." And what brings about this world peace? Coca-Cola.

We spend our money on things that satisfy not, while people in Haiti starve.

In the parable of the rich man and Lazarus, what was the sin of the rich man? It doesn't say he committed adultery, or lied, or cheated. It doesn't say he did anything evil, except he fared sumptuously every day while Lazarus sat at his gates suffering. The Scripture says that when the rich man died, he went to hell.

Then I hear such arrogant statements in men's Bible classes as "You can't help people who are too stupid to help themselves." I've been to Haiti, and they *are* stupid. Why? Because when they were infants their diets were so poor that their brains never developed. And there are hundreds of thousands of people in the Caribbean area who are mentally retarded because they were undernourished.

Yes, they are stupid, but the Day of Judgment is coming. And we as the white middle class will be held accountable. The first thing we must do is repent. That's where it begins. The secret is not in coming up with some new technique, some new sociological insight, some new trick of the trade. The key is repentance.

One of the classes I taught at the University of Pennsylvania had seven hundred students. The discussion was becoming very cynical one day, so I asked, "Is there anybody at all that you respect?" One student raised his hand and said, "Yes, Albert Schweitzer."

That interested me, primarily because I don't like Schweitzer's theology. Evangelicals can't exactly be thrilled when they read his *Quest for the Historical Jesus*. So I asked the student, "What impressed you about this man?" But I didn't have to ask. I knew why. Here was a man who had wealth, power, and fame. He was one of the greatest interpreters of Bach's music and a renowned theologian. But at the age of forty, he sold everything and went into the interior of Africa to serve the poor.

One doesn't have to approve of his theology or his ministry. Only one thing impressed that cynical group of university students: not his theology, but his willingness to sacrifice.

We must understand what the cross is all about. Jesus did not say, "I give you a new theological insight that people will be drawn to. If you eloquently preach, they will be turned on." Instead, he said, "If I be lifted up, I will draw all men unto myself."

What the inner city is looking for is not more sociologically keen theologians. What it's looking for is a generation of people who will accept their own crosses, who will lift up Jesus Christ, and who are willing to pay the price.

Three

URBAN CHURCH/
URBAN POOR

John Perkins

TWO OR THREE YEARS AGO, I was asked to spend a week at Denver University talking about the poor. I used Luke 4:18 as my basic passage of Scripture, in which Jesus says, "The Spirit of the Lord is upon me, because he hath anointed me to preach the gospel to the poor."

Most of the students were rich, suburban, and white. About the middle of that week, one young lady came to me and said, "Brother Perkins, I believe you are over-emphasizing this whole idea of the poor. I think Jesus really meant 'poor in spirit' in this passage."

I replied, "Jesus knew how to say 'spirit.' If you turn to the Gospel of Matthew, Jesus says, 'Blessed are the poor in spirit.' But in Luke 4, he meant the poor."

John M. Perkins
   Mr. Perkins is president of Voice of Calvary Ministries. He is the author of Let Justice Roll Down *and* A Quiet Revolution.

People are poor basically because they are disenfranchised and powerless. The whole idea of Jesus coming into the world, and the whole idea of the church, is to give us power and a solution to our problems.

The Bible says that Jesus, "though he was rich, yet for your sakes he became poor, that ye through his poverty might be rich" (2 Cor. 8: 9). We in turn can through him, empower those who are poor. That is why Jesus could say that all power on heaven and earth was in his hands. He was telling us we could share that power with him, down here on earth as his people. We can regain our identity as the people of God when we share His power in liberating people.

FINDING OUR IDENTITY

The first thing we must do is find our identity as the people of God. We have lost our prophetic voice, because we have lost an understanding of what it means to be the church. Once we have found our identity as God's people, then we can speak to the system.

The church was to be the replacement of Jesus Christ's body on earth in a local community; we were to live out God's life again, to take up where he left off. But we have lost our sense of community. When Jesus talked about our being the light of the world, he wasn't talking about us as individuals; he was talking about that collective Body of people who were to be his life in the world.

We begin to see ourselves as being the people of God once we receive Jesus Christ as Savior. Then we are all baptized into this one universal Body. That is an act of the Spirit of God. But God will not act apart from us once we have been placed into that body—he wants us to create anew his Body in a local community.

The first chapters of Revelation include letters to seven churches in seven different cities in Asia Minor. Many of them had problems and weaknesses, but they still belonged to Christ; he himself was in their midst, enabling them to do the greater work Jesus said would happen after he went to the Father. He was talking about how he could come alive in different communities all over the world.

The whole history of the early church was that, over and over again, groups of people would come to believe the gospel message and then Christ's Body would come alive in that community. Once we understand that we are the people of God and find our identity in a local community as the people of God, then we are open to be empowered by God's Spirit. God can work through his Spirit and give us gifts. But while the gifts are given to us individually, they are not to be used as our own individual toys. They are given to be used within the Body so that the Body might come alive in the local community.

The first work of the Spirit of God is to teach us the Word of God. Some people get so carried away with the fringe benefits of the Spirit that they lose the whole idea of the work of the Spirit, which is to empower us to do God's will and to do it within the context of the church.

When we lose the understanding of the gospel, we end up with two churches in the world: a liberal church and an evangelical church. Neither of these is complete, and they both get energy and enthusiasm out of criticizing each other. Unfortunately, the poor have been the victims of that fight.

The evangelical church believes that the gospel is primarily a proclamation, and they talk a lot about getting out the Word. The liberals don't believe so much in the proclamation as they do in good works, in manifestation.

But the gospel is both a proclamation and a manifestation. The gospel is making visible the love of God. The death of Jesus Christ on the cross was God's way of making his love visible to the world so we could understand that he loves us. We who preach the gospel not only have the responsibility to proclaim it but also to be the presence of God in the world so the people can both hear what we say and see our work.

We are not saved by our work. But other people are saved because of our work, because they see our work. That is what Jesus meant when he told us to let our light shine before men so they could see our good works and glorify our Father in heaven (Matt. 5:16).

As I go around the country, it seems to me that people view the primary purpose of the gospel as making church members. The purpose of the gospel is to get people saved. The purpose of the gospel is to reconcile people to God, to each other, and to do it in one Body. The history of mankind is that man broke a relationship with God, but God was in Christ, reconciling the world to himself. And because he has given us the ministry of reconciliation, we are to take God's place on earth and reconcile people to God. We are to do that in one Body across racial, economic, and cultural barriers and lines. That is the glory of the gospel—for God to call out of the world black and white, Jew and Gentile alike, transforming them into a new people who are God's new people and love each other.

Sometimes white folks say to me, "Can white people win black folks as good as black folks can win black folks?"

And I say to them, "That is a racist question." We have been commanded to go into all the world and preach the gospel to every creature. What causes us to ask that kind of question is exactly the evidence that we have been damaged, because God already commanded us to do it. And God would not command us to do something that he has not given us the power to carry out. What has happened is that we have adjusted the gospel into our culture and traditions, so the gospel has lost its power.

PRINCIPLES OF THE QUIET REVOLUTION

Let me give you the three principles of the quiet revolution, which are applicable to any community, rural or urban.

First, the church has to relocate itself in the area of need. God visited the world; he didn't just send a messenger. He located himself in the world; he moved to the area of need. The church in the city has got to live among the poor and find its identity among the poor. We cannot just come in from the suburbs with Christmas baskets, or commute back and forth. We are to be the Body of Christ where people are oppressed.

Second, we have to believe *again* that the goal of the gospel is to reconcile people to God across racial, economic, and social barriers. Directly connected with this is the third principle of the quiet revolution, redistributing wealth. We must come up with new ways to redistribute wealth to people in need. We have to face the fact that our present economic system is creating the poor and the conditions they live in. It is going to be much more difficult in the future for Christians to convince the poor that they really are Christians—because of their life-styles. We must come up with new ways of living in order to make certain that other people can live better.

Urban people are poor basically because they are disenfranchised; they have no equity in society. The American system is based on ownership, individual ownership, and we have created a class of people without a sense of ownership. The church is going to have to begin to empower that underclass. The idea of the gospel is to burn through that class system and bring people together, redirecting our resources and energies toward the poor.

Empowering the poor does not mean taking money from the rich and giving it to the poor. If you would do that, and leave the present system of ownership intact, the rich would have their money back tomorrow, because the poor would go out and buy things like Cadillacs and suede shoes. Instead, the poor must have the power that makes wealth and controls wealth.

One to three percent of the American people own the means of production that generates 69 percent of the wealth in our country. Another 3-9 percent of the people help the first group control the means of production. Then there is the middle class, people who make twenty-five to fifty-thousand dollars a year, probably the most reactionary class in American society. Then comes the working class, and below them, the poor, the disenfranchised, who own nothing.

We have to discover how to overcome this economic disenfranchisement. Our welfare programs are further retarding the people because they are not being given the dignity of being creative. Our system is giving jobs to the poor that demean them and take away their dignity. People need to be able to be proud of what they do.

Our society, based on ownership, has taken away from the poor the ability to own property. Instead, we place them in public housing. The reason people destroy housing is that they have no sense of ownership.

All public housing should be cooperative housing. That wouldn't be hard. All we would have to do is move them in, give them a deed, and let them start paying in equity. The interest rate might go something like this: for the first five years, 1 percent; for the next five years, 2 percent; after that, 5 percent. That would allow people to immediately start having some equity.

Hosea Moran, in his book *Marxists and the Bible,* says the underclass is the most perfect form of slavery yet contrived by man. The key to the slavery is that they hold and cherish the ideals of their oppressors. We have all become consumers.

What we must do is change our values, and the church must lead the way.

The evangelical church has to find its identity; as a matter of fact, it has to find a *new* identity. It can no longer be neutral; it has to be aggressive. The evangelical has too long been identified with the rich and the oppressor in American society. When Governor Wallace stood in the schoolhouse door to block black kids, he was rewarded with an honorary doctor's degree from a fundamentalist college because of his noble stand for separation in the classroom. In 1954, when blacks were beginning to get enfranchised politically, the evangelical church was nowhere to be seen. It wasn't really a matter of joining their team during the civil rights movement, because the evangelicals did not even have a team on the field.

Today, good white Christians sometimes ask me how they can win black people. The first thing I tell them is "When the black folks move into your community, don't move out. Then you'll get to know some and get to love them, because they'd be there." What happens, though, is that blacks move in and whites move out, and six months later, the whites send their kids back to the neighborhood with the Four Spiritual Laws and try to tell those folks that God loves them. The black people cannot help but wonder why those Christians didn't show love when they had a real opportunity to do so.

The evangelical church must find its identity as the people of God and become a community of love. We must love our neighbor as we love ourselves; we must move in among the poor and identify with them; we must empower the poor and disenfranchised—by bringing them Jesus Christ. It won't do any good to go to the poor with the idea of developing another program. We need to raise up a community of people, a fellowship. Then as these people find and claim their identity, we help establish programs that fit their needs so that they will not be continually poor.

When we become the community of God's people, we will not be just a prophetic voice condemning society. We will be a model of what society ought to be.

Four

DEVELOPING BLACK LEADERSHIP IN WHITE DENOMINATIONS

James White

THE DEVELOPMENT OF LEADERS is not a mystery. It is a process that depends on the challenges and aspirations that confront a given group at a given time in history. Leaders are produced by their social group. Only after we face the truth of this fact can we begin to understand what it takes to see black leadership emerge in white denominations.

Dr. Martin Luther King, Jr., was a product of the South, and specifically the southern black church. No other group in the world could have produced the genius of Dr. King. He was a direct extension of that group. He was molded by wrestling with the group's difficulties as they were perceived and defined.

James B. White

Mr. White is currently holding a double appointment as assistant professor of sociology and theology at Trinity Christian College. He served as pastor to the Manhattan Christian Reformed Church for 8½ years.

Through the activities of that group, he refined and honed the ability God gave him. The group determined what was important, and Dr. King bent himself to doing it.

Malcolm X, on the other hand, came from the North. At that particular time in history, if a hero were to be produced out of the northern black community, he would have had to have been a Malcolm X—because the kinds of issues the community was concerned about would have produced nothing else. Malcolm X had the kind of abilities that the community cherished and encouraged.

Every group must struggle with its own problems, defining and explaining to itself the nature of the challenge that confronts it. The black community in America must define and explain racism *for itself*— never mind the white folks. A little black child has to be told by the Afro-American community what racism is, how it looks, and how it behaves.

Hall, Cross, and Friedal, three black psychologists, have developed a theoretical model of the four phases of development of black awareness. The first is the preencounter stage, in which the person believes, having been taught from the wider community, that this world is and should be run by European Americans. In the second stage, the encounter stage, the black person begins to believe that the world should be interpreted from the black perspective. The third stage is the immersion stage, when the black person involves himself in a world of blackness, undergoing a sense of liberation from whiteness. In the fourth stage, which is called internalization, the black person achieves a sense of inner security, a satisfaction with himself or herself, and a concern and sympathy that reaches to all oppressed people.

These are the lessons that the community teaches. The young child learns them at the knees of grandma and uncle and neighbor and church. Through this process, the community produces its own heroes. The group recognizes and confirms the talents of a youngster, offers him encouragement, and builds structures to develop and cultivate his talent.

Eventually, the group legitimizes this person as a leader. No leader can exercise his or her function unless the legitimate right to lead is acknowledged by the community. But his acceptance is in some ways a foregone conclusion, since the community has been shaping the leader in its own image all along.

DO WHITE DENOMINATIONS WANT BLACK LEADERS?

White denominations that claim to want black leaders in their midst cannot ignore these basic facts of sociology. It takes more than ordination to make a leader. A similar problem exists in professional football, which only now is beginning to have black quarterbacks. Why? Because black players can't throw the ball or plan offensive strategy in the huddle? Hardly. But leadership has to be acknowledged and supported by the group.

And herein lies the difficulty: which group?

The existence of two groups is undeniable. In the greater Chicago area, for example, there are 27 black and 12 Hispanic United Methodist churches out of a total of 151. Out of 120 Lutheran churches, 12 are interracial or black and 2 are Hispanic. Out of 133 United Presbyterian churches, 18 are black and 2 are Hispanic. Out of 170 United Churches of Christ, 12 are black or interracial and 4 are Hispanic. And in each case, the groups are separated geographically. The black and Hispanic churches are concentrated in the heart of the city, while the white churches form a large ring around the outside.

We have a problem in our churches, because if leaders are nurtured and molded by their groups, we cannot expect that black leadership will succeed in directing an essentially white group, or vice versa.

THE MAKING OF ONE GROUP

The primary reason we are two groups is that we do not share enough of one another's history. Black psychologists have been doing some study on this matter (see *Black Psychology*, edited by Reginald Jones) and have made a distinction between belonging to a group *by behavior* and belonging to a group *by history*. For example, two middle-class people, a black person and a white person, may share many behavioral characteristics that are the same, especially in public. But two black people, one perhaps very poor and the other a genuine millionaire, have a deeper belongingness; they share the same history. The historical dimension, the psychologists argue, is what makes the group a people.

The white denominations and the black community do not share enough of one another's history to be a people. When we talk about the people of God, we misuse the word *people* unless we are talking about a common history.

Since there are two groups, how can white denominations hope to develop black leadership from the Afro-American community? Of course there are some blacks in white denominations, but these people are the expression of the black ideal of church union. The black church has always maintained that the Body of Christ is indivisible, while white denominations have all too often felt that separate development was good. The black church has never entertained that notion; one of its ideals has always been the communion of the saints. My grandmamma used to say, "Oh, you know, son, there is an awful lot of prejudice in this world, and sometimes you have to be careful, because it can be dangerous. But in the church we are all brothers and sisters." My career in the ministry is an expression of the attempt to fulfill her ideal.

Some white denominations have attempted to establish programs of recruitment, but then the question arises, "Recruitment to what?" How can anyone recruit except from an attitude of superiority that says, "You ought to want to be over here where I am." And all too often the reason is not because the white group is so great and exciting and vital and prophetic—but just because of *who* it is. It doesn't work.

So what is the answer? There must be one group, so that there is one definition of the problems, challenges, and difficulties that confront the Church of Jesus Christ.

Walking down the road from Selma to Montgomery, I remember looking around a swampy area on the right and hill country on the left. I said to myself, "You know, it's dangerous out here. Someone could be murdered and never again found." Then I looked at the man walking beside me, and I observed to myself, "This is a white man. And those troops that have been called out to protect us, but are flying Dixie flags and spitting on us—they're spitting on him, too. This man is sharing my danger, my problem; we have at this point a shared history of experience; we have defined and described the problem *together*. We walk down this road *to-*

gether." He was a lawyer, but he represented no larger body; he was there on his own. And I kept wondering if Dr. King's movement would pull in the denominations. Would it gain enough momentum to sway various church bodies, so that they too would share in the danger, the difficulties, the consequences, the fate?

Sharing works the other way as well. We black folks have to share the burdens of the white denominations. I suffer in the black community because my denomination did not take a very strong stand on the South African issue. The problems of the suburbs become mine just as the problems of the city are those of my white brothers. I sometimes tell them, "You know, just from a very selfish point of view, you ought to make sure there are strong churches in the big cities, because when your child runs away, you'd better be able to pick up the phone and say, 'Reverend, he is five-foot-two and blonde, can you catch him at the bus station?' " Seriously, that is a ministry, and any urban pastor shares that kind of burden.

In addition to shared burdens, we must have aspirations, hopes, and dreams, which lead us to shared activities. Malcolm X said, "If I can reach the men, I will have the women." He was not being a male chauvinist; he simply recognized that the woman in poverty usually places her aspirations in her children. She can come to church and wait patiently for ten years, because her hopes are embedded in her children as they grow into maturity. But the black man must fulfill his aspirations in himself *now.* He can't wait ten years; he is not yet ready to say he hasn't made it and is a failure. He is not ready to sublimate and transfer all of his hopes and dreams to his children. He is still operating; he is still in business; he is now-oriented.

If he walks into a church and finds that it shares those

aspirations and dreams *now*, he feels at home. Therefore, the acid test of the white denomination is: Do you
have the black man? How strong is your men's fellowship? What are you doing for them?

Malcolm X made the Muslim movement a men's
movement, "and you ain't going to stop me," he said.
"I'm going to run over the church; all they have is the
women, and they don't understand."

When we share one another's aspirations as well as
burdens and history, then we will share one another's
faith. The result will finally be the existence of *one
group*—and then the conditions will be ripe for leadership development. Then God will bless in an abundant
way that goes beyond our imagining.

I will say again that the development of leaders depends on our understanding and coming to a consensus
about the challenges that confront a group at a given
time in history. When God came to Abraham, he was
already a leader of a people. They were more than a
group; they had shared a common history. God made
him a promise, "I know you are the head of a people, but
one day, I'm going to make you into a nation."

A group that shares its experiences and aspirations
becomes a people. They are not a racial entity; they are a
historical development. And if they are successful, they
become a nation. God said he was going to give his
people a land. Anybody can be a tribe of people, but
Abraham was made to understand that his people had to
have land, to take part of God's creation.

We, the Church, face a similar challenge today. Right
now we are two groups. May God help us to become one
people, and then to seize this world and all its systems
and become a nation. And as that happens,
leadership—black and white—will arise to take us for-
ward in unity to a new day.

Five

CHURCH GROWTH IN BLACK CONGREGATIONS

William Bentley and Willie Jemison

William Bentley:

WHAT ARE THE DISTINCTIVES of church growth in the black community? First, it must be recognized that the black community is not one but many different communities, and that applies to church traditions as well.

The vast majority of black Christians today are members of churches with black structures. It was not always this way, however. Almost without exception, the black church started out within a white structure. Religious worship was, for the most part, proscribed; we could not participate, and certainly not by ourselves. When our ancestors first came here, it can be pretty well assumed they did not know much about Jesus Christ. A few slaves

William H. Bentley

Mr. Bentley is the pastor of the Calvary Bible Church in Chicago, a community relations worker with the Illinois Department of Public Aid, and actively involved with the National Black Evangelical Association, serving as national president from 1970 through 1976.

may have, but for the most part our ancestors were devotees of the traditional religions of West Africa.

They were introduced to Christ in various ways. Sometimes they backed into it; at other times they absorbed it indirectly; sometimes they were direct objects of evangelism; but there came a time when, although perhaps the majority of the slaves were not Christians, the Christian religion had a more profound influence on them than any other set of beliefs. The result was that even though not all black people were religious, the Christian religion began to assume a dominant role in their lives.

For one thing, they were cut off from their religion of the past, and they were not able to enter into or justify their present condition. Many people felt that if their African god were really so strong, he would not have allowed them to be taken into slavery. The conclusion for those people, then, was to junk their previous gods and look for a new set of beliefs.

At any rate, the Christian presence began to make itself felt among the black people, and different traditions of worship began to develop among them. If the slaves belonged to people of high status, such as Presbyterians, Episcopalians, or Congregationalists, the slaves absorbed the worship characteristics of those groups. It wasn't until after the Great Awakening that the Baptists and Methodists began to exert the kind of influence that eventually almost transformed the whole religious outlook of black people.

In the North, the situation was somewhat different than in the South. Because there were more freed persons and not as many slaves, the restrictions on worship were not as tight, although they were still there. In the South, however, soon after the rebellions led by Nat Turner and others, blacks were prevented from gathering together. Two or three black people could not be together unless a white man were present. That, of course, marked the development of their religious practices as well as social life.

Probably the incident of most far-reaching significance in the whole history of the black church was the founding of the African Methodist Episcopal Church—notice the word *African,* a deliberate choice. This church was started out of the Saint George Methodist Church, which was *the* church at that time for Methodists in America, and which a small minority of blacks—both slaves and freed—attended.

From the journals of Richard Allen, I have learned of a strong cultural nationalism among the blacks of that time, and they chose to call themselves Africans. The process of slavery had not broken the strong cultural ties; they retained an ethnic identity. Their reasons for leaving and starting the new church were not purely racial, although that was the precipitating factor. The immediate cause for their quitting the Methodist church was their being forbidden to take part in the prayer service.

But there were deeper causes: there were cultural expressions denied them and certain traditions they were not free to express. So they got up and left after the prayer meeting incident and started a church based on ethnic identity, an ethnic approach to the religion of Jesus Christ. (If we stop and think about it, that is all Christianity has ever been from the very beginning—a series of ethnic approaches.)

In the black urban church, particularly the church in a black structure, we can still trace the value of and the preference for the ethnic approach and interpretation. More than 90 percent of black Christians worship in structures that are predominantly black. National Baptist conventions probably account for seven or eight million blacks. Black Methodists are another million and a half, and the Church of God in Christ and other related Pentecostal groups might add up to ten million.

The fact that 90 percent of all black Christians worship within black structures determines their religious needs; that setting calls for specific responses.

Prior to the revolutionary rhetoric of the 1960s, black Christians in white structures were not particularly noted for their militance or ethnic identity. But the sixties radicalized the black caucuses within the major white denominations so that they were then identified without question with the majority of other blacks.

Willie Jemison:

AT LEAST FIVE ELEMENTS are necessary for church growth in black congregations: a relevant message, a holistic ministry, a strong pulpit ministry, an exciting worship hour, and a caring pastor.

First, the relevant message. For me, that entails what we think of as black theology. It is no different in the basic interpretations, but the illustrations are different, because we take into account the people whom we are addressing and the community in which we are involved. People have to be able to identify with our message and our concern. That is part of ethnicity of worship—we *are* different, and not just in color. Some folks don't want to accept that, but in a worship service, we just don't act the same.

Second, we must have *a holistic message;* we cannot

Willie B. Jemison

Mr. Jemison is pastor of the Oakdale Covenant Church. He is a committee member of the minister's division of Operation PUSH (People United to Save Humanity) and a member of the Urban Ministry Task Force of the Covenant Church Central Conference.

afford the luxury of winning souls to the exclusion of winning the whole person. We cannot dissect a man, focusing on his spiritual or emotional needs while ignoring his educational, housing, and economic needs.

We may not have a church member as the principal of the local school, but we have a responsibility to see that somebody is there who can really do that job. And if the wrong person's there, then we have to move them—not because of color, but because he doesn't know how to do the job. Recently a dozen black preachers stood in the door at a local school and told the principal he had to go. The community had been trying to get rid of him for five years; we stood there for one morning, and that was that—he didn't come back.

We need to be visible on the high-school and college levels of education, too. We sometimes have to say some harsh-sounding things to college professors and college presidents within the white structure. We have to cut through the rhetoric and flowery language and, sometimes, use some very crude terms until they finally get the message. We have to tell them we don't want our kids going to their schools and finally leaving their campuses not knowing anything about their own identity, because all the models they see on campus are white. Sometimes, the white structure is careful not to say anything bad about us while at the same time making sure we're not there in any ways that could make a difference. It is another case of "benign neglect."

Thirdly, church growth in the black community comes from *a strong pulpit ministry.* There are at least four kinds of black preachers: the hacker, who usually comes from the South; the whooper, whose poetical language can ascend and descend the chromatic scale beautifully; the hollerer, who is like a whooper, except that he doesn't have a tune (I fit this category); and finally, the exciting lecturer, who doesn't have the other verbal gifts the others have, but he says it enthusiastically. None of these are right or wrong; they are all equally acceptable in our community, and all will help stimulate church growth.

A strong pulpit ministry means that you have to say it like you mean it. The people don't care how you say it, and they probably don't even care what denominational shingle you hang out, as long as you can tell the story. They don't want to know what Bonhoeffer or Tillich says; they only ask, "Preacher, what does the Lord tell you to tell us?" It is important to believe what you're saying; if you don't, then don't say it.

A black preacher can be having all sorts of problems within his congregation, with all the organizations and individuals fighting each other. But when he gets up and preaches on Sunday morning, the whole thing can come together; the church solidifies, simply because he told the story.

Then there has to be *an exciting worship hour.* I say "hour," but in the black church, we don't use clocks— we use calendars! My church is now 97 percent black, but on any given Sunday, a number of white folks will be there. They come from all over, just because they're in town and they know something's happening at our church, even though the service is usually two hours long. Something's moving. Our worship time needs to include all kinds of music: singing from the hymnal, singing from tradition, and singing solid gospel music.

Finally, church growth in black congregations necessitates *a caring pastor.* We have to be where the people are, sharing their joys and sorrows. The black pastor acts as the hub of the wheel, holding all the spokes together. If we get out of this place, the wheel does not roll and everything falls down.

These are some of the specific elements that cause the black church to grow. They are not especially new; they have been with us since early times. They will serve us successfully in the future as well.

Six

TOWARD AN URBAN CHURCH STRATEGY

Donald L. Benedict

ANY ATTEMPT TO BUILD an urban church strategy must begin with an analysis of the missionary situation. As Reinhold Niebuhr and Paul Tillich used to say, "We are at the end of an era and on the threshold of a world powerless to be born." To understand what it means to be at the end of the Protestant era is the first step toward understanding the missionary situation. The identification of the Protestant ethic with the individualism of the American economic frontier finds limited acceptance in an era of limited resources and concentrated corporate power. Protestantism, with its emphasis on the individual's personal relation to God, has always had difficulty in the city. It has always been more at home in the village or rural area where individual effort and volun-

Donald L. Benedict
Mr. Benedict is the executive director of the Community Renewal Society, an urban mission agency related to the United Church of Christ. He was one of the founders of the East Harlem Protestant parish concept in New York City.

tary association were necessary for survival.

To know the missionary situation in the city, one has to understand the growth of American cities. By and large our cities grew out of economic necessity rather than planning. They emerged and grew primarily at points where rivers or lakes or raw materials made the location attractive to the expanding industrial enterprise. At the early stages of the industrial revolution, the need for unskilled laborers to perform ever more simple, routine functions brought millions of immigrants to our cities seeking work. Likewise, the invention of the cotton gin and mechanized farm equipment pushed thousands of unskilled laborers off the farms and into our cities. Cities grew because they were transportation, communication, and industrial centers. They were needed to forge the industrial enterprise. Art, culture, and music really came as an afterthought.

But now, American cities, as we know them, are not economically feasible. Without subsidy, either federal, state, or local, most would now be inoperable and probably bankrupt. Cities, like many aspects of our industrial society, have been a part of our throwaway culture. The cities house a large proportion of the vast number of people who live in poverty. Cities have lost their tax base. Businesses no longer have to be in the city since now most business transactions can be carried on by computer and television technology.

Likewise, cities are no longer needed as a source of unskilled labor. Modern technology has eliminated large numbers of unskilled workers. Many manufacturing plants have, over the last decade or so, systematically moved away from cities into the suburbs, rural areas, and frequently overseas, wherever there is cheaper labor, lower taxes, or other economic advantages.

Cities are coming more and more to reflect the growing gap of income in America. In biblical terms the rich are getting richer and the poor poorer. Some cities are becoming huge slums surrounded by affluence. Some are being divided into neighborhoods of affluence and poverty. One out of six families in our country is now on welfare, and one out of three households makes under $9,500 a year.

This economic classification that is intensifying in urban neighborhoods has profound ramifications for urban church strategy. We must face not only racial transition but extreme economic transition. Some sections of our larger cities are being rehabilitated with singles and childless couples who are prepared to take a new lease on city life. For the most part they may remain childless and will not require an educational system, or they may be affluent enough to afford private schools. When neighborhoods begin to attract the more affluent, the poor are again excluded as land values, taxes, and rents increase. This means that more and more city churches and neighborhoods will reflect economic and racial segregation and will require a long-term strategy on the part of mainline Protestant denominations.

Further economic segregation may be increased by the energy shortage, which makes near-downtown property very desirable. This trend is now apparent in Chicago, San Francisco, Washington, D.C., and other cities. Denominations that have sold or abandoned older downtown church buildings will now find it necessary to rebuild in order to accommodate the new middle and upper class urbanite. Conversely, the energy crisis, limited mortgage money, and the high cost of housing may retard somewhat the economic and racial transition of communities. As long as our current system of land and housing development remains profitable, however, we will continue to be confronted with transitional communities.

As our society becomes less upwardly mobile (due to lack of energy and limited natural resources), we will experience more economic and class stratification, and large sections of our cities and certain suburbs will remain inhabited by low income groups. If these groups are to be given the opportunity of joining mainline denominations, considerable ongoing subsidies by the denominations will be required.

There are some other trends that are apt to have an effect on urban church strategy. The increased participation of women in the work force (43 percent) is related not only to women's liberation but also to economic necessity. Almost half of the working women are heads of households. Among working wives, one-third live with husbands earning less than $7,000 annually, more than half with men earning less than $10,000 a year—in a society in which $10,000 is now an austerity budget for a family of four according to U.S. Chamber of Commerce. Therefore, the loss of one of the incomes in these families can lead to the loss of a home. There is no doubt that women in the work force have had an effect on the amount of volunteer time available to city churches.

Likewise, the two-job or moonlighting syndrome has reduced the amount of volunteer time available to the local urban church. Similarly, the suburban church and some high-income city churches have felt the impact of the time constraints of global managers, both men and women, whose national and international travel schedules make participation in local events and community building almost impossible. In fact, it is exceedingly difficult for most urban dwellers to identify any meaningful community of which they are a part. In the absence of a real human or religious community, we have witnessed all over America a deep search for individual identity. The fragmentation of our culture has turned us inward in a search for a mystical selfhood. This mood is currently reflected in our churches.

Yet, is it not true that faith begins with concern for the poor and outcast? Is not the Kingdom to be inhabited by those who see the face of Christ in the suffering of people? In Matthew 25, the Kingdom is prepared for us as we give food to the hungry, give drink to the thirsty, welcome the stranger, clothe the naked, and visit the sick and those in prisons. This concern for the welfare of the least of those among us seems to be the benchmark of the faith. Those who respond positively will move into the eternal life and those who fail to respond are to go away into eternal punishment. It appears to be a clear separation of sheep and goats.

Again in Luke 4, reporting Jesus' first public utterance in the synagogue at Nazareth, the statement of mission is clearly delineated: "to set at liberty those who are oppressed."

These biblical references strongly suggest that faith is forged out of action and reflection on the needs of the poor and oppressed. There are many roles that the church has played in relation to the poor and oppressed, but in our day the prophetic role of the churches is critical. In a culture devoid of transcendence and concerned primarily with hedonistic self-gratification, the church must speak the truth in love. This prophetic stance should determine the basic strategy of the urban church both in its congregational and judicatory expressions.

Obviously, each church and each judicatory (denominational organization) must develop a strategy consonant with its needs and perceptions. However, I would like to suggest five major areas of program development that I consider crucial in light of the current urban missionary situation.

1. *Institutional survival.* Judicatories must develop strategies so that churches in areas of racial and economic transition can survive as well as those in areas of affluence. As long as American cities are racially and economically segregated, it will be necessary for denominational leadership to begin redistributing resources from churches with "market potential" to those churches with low and moderate incomes. Denominations with connectional judicatories, such as Catholic, Methodist, Presbyterian, Episcopalian, and Lutheran forms of organization, will find this cooperation easier to attain, although it will require an overall strategy from the denominational level. For churches with freer polity, such as Baptists, United Churches of Christ, and interdenominational congregations, more informal and covenantal relationships between the wealthy and the poor will be necessary.

Churches facing economic and racial transition are faced with problems that appear at first hand to be insurmountable. Walter E. Ziegenhals, director of the "Churches-in-Transition" project of the Community Renewal Society and United Church of Christ in Chicago, sums up these factors when he says:

> The congregation in a community facing or undergoing racial transition is confronted with a complex of problems. Normally these include such factors as: aging and declining membership; a diminishing financial base; insufficient or inadequate leadership; racial fears (as well as ethnic, cultural and class fears); movement of membership away from the church building;

inability to understand the interrelation between community's fate and the church's future; estrangement from new neighbors; concern with local issues to the exclusion of metropolitan trends; and difficulty in defining the mission of the church beyond meeting the needs of the present membership.

The church in economic and racial transition is not a new phenomenon. Oscar Handlin noted these lines of population settlement in New York City in the 1880s. Every denomination is faced with this fact of city life.

It is difficult to predict where transitional areas will appear, whether in the city or in certain fringe suburbs. However, one thing is clear: the continuous movement to escape the poor will continue unabated as long as the market forces determine the structure and locality of city neighborhoods. Likewise there seems to be little hope of race diminishing as a major factor in the development of transitional neighborhoods. It is clear that few individual church strategies will be successful without the full participation and support of judicatories.

2. *Theological reflection on the cultural milieu.* We need to reflect on the way in which we have accommodated the gospel to our culture. Christian values are difficult to identify in the current life-style of American Christians. Even though life-style changes may not come from discussion alone, pastors and laity must see this dialogue as a serious and long term quest for a fundamental reorientation of their faith.

Judicatories have the responsibility of securing adequate resource people for this endeavor. We must ask serious questions about the relation of the gospel to a hedonistic, instant gratification culture as well as economic, social, and political questions dealing with justice and the use of God-given natural resources. In a nation in which a stable GNP will increase the level of greed, the question of justice may well become a survival issue. Where else in our culture can these questions find serious consideration?

3. *Race as an all-pervasive issue.* Discrimination against blacks and Latinos has become more subtle and complex than it was prior to the sixties. Nonetheless, it remains. In Chicago, the issue of race permeates almost every problem in the city—school desegregation, police and fire department discriminatory hiring practices, allocation of ambulances equipped with telemetry devices, housing practices, insurance rates, and redlining.

Many churchmen seem to be stunned that their efforts of the sixties only succeeded in opening a few knotholes to blacks and Latinos. The fact is that we must now prepare for a major assault on institutional racism, especially if the Bakke case wipes out affirmative action.

My own experience indicates that independent investigative journalism on institutional racism can have an immediate and profound effect. A monthly newsletter published by a judicatory can bring to public attention the current state of race relations in a community.

For the last five years the Community Renewal Society has published *The Chicago Reporter*, a monthly newsletter on racial issues. The impact of this publication has been enormous. It has continued to systematically publish the facts on race—with little or no commentary. Since each issue is picked up extensively by the mass media, the research carried on by these reporters gets wide coverage. We have seen the policies of law firms and insurance companies changed. We have laid the groundwork for lawsuits charging the misuse of funds for low-income children by the board of education. We most recently witnessed the resignation of the Chicago fire commissioner after a story on the abundance of fire deaths in Chicago.

Presbyteries or synods are capable of using this tool to bring to light the institutional racism that seems to be alive and well in America.

4. *Development of alternative Christian education.* Public education in most of our cities is a disgrace. While the current condition of education cannot be laid totally at the doorsteps of our public schools, the current bureaucratic structure of most schools makes meaning-ful change difficult. Most parents feel hopeless and helpless about making any impact on current public education.

Yet, we must realize that the problems of our schools are due to a host of other causative factors. Wholesome families, proper health care, nutrition, positive work models, and available jobs at the end of the education process are all contributing factors to motivation for learning. Yet after taking all these factors into consid-eration, most of us must conclude that public school students, especially in low-income areas, are not receiv-ing an adequate education. Furthermore, the values transmitted through public education have little to do with the Christian faith. For all intents and purposes, we are dealing with an alien culture. I propose, therefore, that we develop an alternative Christian school that deals constructively with integration and quality educa-tion, and at the same time makes an attempt to transmit Christian values.

I am aware that this move may have a negative effect on public education (especially if these private schools become popular). However, it may be that competition is the only way to checkmate the present educational bureaucracy. It would not be the first time Christians have developed educational systems to communicate the values inherent in the faith. The development of these church schools will, of course, be greatly enhanced if Congress provides a tax deduction for private schools.

Many inner-city churches are strategically located to provide school space. Finances would be difficult, but such schools might even involve parents through direct participation, which would certainly enhance the educational process. These schools in inner-city churches would also provide a positive program of outreach into the community.

5. *Unemployment and the future of work.* Unemployment and underemployment have become America's number one problem. Certainly one of the major consequences of unemployment and underemployment is that people in certain areas of the city simply do not have adequate income. In order to correct this deficiency in employment income, we resort to all sorts of government subsidies for housing, health, education, and public assistance. Government transfer payments take the place of meaningful work at an adequate income. Current strategies indicate that nearly six million persons, disproportionately black, women, and teenagers are being denied the right to earn a living. Millions more work full time for pay that is below the subsistence level established by the Labor Department. The right to earn a living is rooted in the biblical faith: the earth was given to all to nurture and enjoy. A denial of work is essentially a denial of the right of access to the land, tools, and resources with which to earn a living. Some are even raising a constitutional question: can all be guaranteed the right to life, liberty, and the pursuit of happiness if, in fact, some are denied the right to earn a living? They say the denial of a job amounts to a denial

of liberty. Such a denial lays the groundwork of a griev-
ance under the First Amendment to the Constitution.

The question of employment for all who are willing
and able to work is a complex issue. The concept itself
raises many questions about inflation, tariffs, interest
rates, work attitudes, and incentives. Yet it is a fundamental issue. Work lies at the heart of meaning in life.
What we *do* gives us our sense of worth. Work is our
means of contributing to the common life. For a person
to be denied work is to be denied an essential part of life.
Recourse to welfare and unemployment compensation
creates a dependency that destroys the human personality.

Presently we are beginning to make the right to earn a
living a matter of guaranteed national policy. There is
some similarity here to the abolition movement in relation to slavery. Many people feel that our economy
cannot absorb full employment just as many slave owners complained that freeing the slaves would ruin the
economy of the South. Nevertheless, no society can long
endure the development of a massive underclass that is
alienated, rootless, and excluded.

This issue will require careful, long-term work on the
part of judicatories. It is an issue for which no quick
solutions are available. Currently the problem is seen
principally as a problem for unskilled black youth and
women, but this will probably change as limited growth
reduces the personnel needs of more traditional
middle-class workers. It can be likened to the narcotics
problem, which first fixed itself on the poor and minority youth and has now become a middle-class
phenomenon as well.

Judicatories will need to begin serious dialogue on
this issue with the unemployed and underemployed.
Some sensitive middle-management people already see

the serious nature of this problem. Coalitions must be drawn together that can systematically work at this issue in an action-reflection dialogue. Research must be carried out on the constitutional and legislative aspects of this problem both at the national and state levels. Criteria must be established to measure the impact of public work programs and governmental job programs on jobs and neighborhoods.

We must recognize that often the work in our society that most needs to be done is in the areas of the city where most of the underemployed are to be found.

Whatever strategy judicatories and local churches pursue, they will be well advised to think clearly about the goals and objectives of that strategy. We are in an age in which the disintegration of our culture presents us with a maze of needs and ills crying out for help. We are all in danger of responding to the need that seems most crucial at the moment. We need to analyze the nature of our cultural disintegration and to ascertain those areas that will be crucial in the long run. We may be well beyond a finger-in-the-dike approach. We may be dealing now with a new reservoir.

PART TWO
The Church
Faces Problems

Seven

CHURCHES IN CHANGING COMMUNITIES

Carl Dudley

SOME OF OUR CHURCHES are grappling with an unusually difficult phenomenon, the American city. Our large cities are perhaps the most culturally unstable urban environments, although there are other cities like them in the world, where the economy has overrun the traditional lines of human relationships.

But somehow the church seems to be ignoring this phenomenon. When we consider church growth, we often spend our time deciding where we will plant new churches. In the Presbyterian church, my own orientation, we rarely look at the fact that we are losing more churches than we are organizing.

To be specific, we Presbyterians abandon two

Carl S. Dudley

Dr. Dudley is professor of church and community of McCormick Theological Seminary. He teaches courses in laity expectations of church membership and the reaction of the church to social issues.

churches in the city for every one we organize in the green suburban pastures. Church growth people spend so much time and technology developing new churches that they rarely look at the urban environment, where most of the established congregations of our historic faith are failing. (Lest that become just a WASP comment, the same basic tendency affects the black and Hispanic churches.) The nation that was once supposed to be a melting pot has become a ladder, and the church provides the rungs.

The urban area is constantly moving from one cultural group to another, from one economic group to another—often from white to black, or from what was once identified as a community, an urban village, into a more heterogeneous area, or from residential to commercial.

I will speak only of racial transition, which is the one I've tried to examine in terms of status and steps, but racial transition has some influence on, and is consistent with, other types of transition.

Often racial transition is taken as a natural recycling of property in the United States, as if there ought to be a trickle-down theory of housing, where homes are originally good for those who can purchase them and then are passed on down to different populations who can use that particular property in various stages of their passage up the American ladder of success. This is an almost uniquely American situation, and the real estate industry has been allowed to manipulate the moments of entry and exit in these areas by the prices and desirability of property. What happens to the people who are caught in this transitional sequence?

Transition can be described as the pressures of push and pull in the American economy, the pull of people who wish to move out where they can have more space, better education, and more of the accoutrements that are possible in the well financed, protected suburbs, and the push of those in the city who are seeking better housing. This push and pull has changed recently as the pressure of migration and the development of the economy has ebbed in northern and eastern cities and increased in southern and western ones.

Basically what happens in this transitional situation is that the community has a breach in the family cycle. Particular units of family housing are no longer replacing themselves. The housing market becomes soft. At that point the real estate industry often moves in to manipulate housing through whatever means are available.

Either the young families are not staying, or the affluent families are moving out, or the families with teenagers no longer feel that this is an appropriate place for them to be. The cycle of renewal that makes a particular community self-generating becomes broken. This pattern of breaking the cycle and moving on happens again and again in urban communities as different groups come in and the property is handed down to lower income groups, a phenomenon Charles Leven calls arbitage. It suggests a turnover of economic groups within racial boundaries that makes it much more difficult to make space sacred for any particular community. It forces upon us the question that is on the horizon: the real issue may not be race but class or success.

How many churches are involved in this transition? In a survey of mainline denominations, 10 percent of the congregations were directly involved; another 10 percent will be involved in the next decade. If a church is to survive this transition, it will cost about $10,000 a year for about ten years, a total of $100,000, or about one third the cost of starting a new church in the suburbs. But somehow the priorities go in the other direction. The church's tendency in transitional areas is to fund social services. I think that risks disaster, and let me suggest why.

In a changing community the established institutions no longer function the way they ought to. There is a sense of institutional impotence. And that's true regardless of the institution. As a matter of fact, churches are often the most insulated of the institutions. If we were the corner store, we would feel the transition sooner and more sharply and have to deal with it perhaps more honestly because we couldn't count on nonresident income.

What happens in a changing community is a loss of turf. The communication and the commerce—all the ways in which funds and goods and services are exchanged throughout the community—are affected. These establishments are threatened by a group of people who no longer see the symbols and the specific things these establishments use as appropriate. It's the small shops and the way people purchase and talk with and through each other that gives a community confidence for survival.

After all, the place of commerce is the place where our gifts are exchanged. When our way of doing things is threatened, we feel it most clearly in the playgrounds and the other pathways that people travel.

Soon there is a loss of resources, a loss of the money that turns over within a community. The only commercial groups that are able to survive the first onslaught of change are those that have a financial base outside—the regional stores of one sort or another and the quick-food chains that often move into transitional areas. What that does is take money out of the community. In a healthy community, it has been estimated that a dollar turns over seventeen times. As the community gets sicker, the sources of turning money over become less and less resident. Hence, both the financial and physical capital is lost.

And so is the trust. What really makes a community work is people knowing each other long enough to trust. Leadership is not simply running meetings or businesses; you must know someone long enough for them to trust you. But the leaders are often the most mobile, and they are the people who are lost first.

If the transition were rational, new people would replace the old. But that is not what happens. After people leave, there is often an increasing vacuum, often vacant housing. Usually the first persons who are different can come and live quite comfortably. One or two families live in a community without any noticeable reaction. But after a time there may develop a space of vacant housing, because the family cycle did not renew itself. It's not just a natural turnover; something strange begins to happen. There is a tipping point that can be anticipated or prevented.

There has been a lot of discussion about where this tipping point really is. Some people say the tipping point is at 10 percent black population; some say 20 percent. Others say it is a ratio between black population and economic income. All those who are sure don't agree. Whatever it is, black becomes important, because it is a visible difference. The strange American psyche is threatened by that difference.

Somebody has suggested that the tipping point in Cicero, which is a somewhat Bohemian community in Chicago that Martin Luther King once tried to march through, is .01 percent. The fact is we don't know what the tipping point will be. It does not even have to happen. As the pressure to move in reduces and the possibility of moving out slows down, the potential of a relatively stable, integrated community seems to increase. However, if there is vacant housing, if the community has lost confidence in itself, and if the real estate industry moves in, there will be a sudden change in the proportion of black and white populations, which is commonly called the tipping point. I've not seen any church or community organization that has successfully prevented the massive onslaught of these forces.

The first people to move in do not necessarily want to see a second wave. Often the first black or Hispanic people, for instance, are the least anxious to see the next black or Hispanic move in.

This lack of acceptance is equally true whether we're talking about the community or the congregation. The idea that the old facilities will accommodate the new families or that the community will remain what it was is also a myth. In most cases, the families are younger and therefore larger. Furthermore, they are often of an increasingly lower economic group and need an increasing number of wage earners in order to pay the inflated prices they have been charged to move in. Therefore the population will increase in the given facilities, which weren't built for larger family use of the electricity, plumbing, schools, or whatever. The pattern of change is really, then, a breakdown of confidence and an increased use of facilities.

Now let's turn to what happens in the congregation. I'd like to believe in the integrated church. I would like to believe that churches being Christian can somehow absorb new people in them. And many congregations honestly say, "Our doors are open." Most of our denominations have affirmations of integration and of how the church will be turned over to new residents as the community changes to a minority group.

Having said all those theologically correct things, yet after looking at about forty-five congregations in the city, I don't know one that didn't think they would survive the transition intact. Congregations assume continuity. They somehow feel that this turf is theirs. "We belong here. It is part of us." And they don't really believe that will change.

As the community changes, the congregation is driven indoors. "This at least is our space. We grew up here, and we felt good about it. You can see it by the 'trophies,' the years of our strength and vitality." They can also point to other churches that have survived transition intact, but they are usually big churches. Or they'll point to ethnic congregations that weren't changed by three waves of people who passed by them. Or to some high-commitment churches that moved into the area when other congregations moved out. They can often say, "Look, that congregation survived, and we can, too."

There is a fundamental reason for their belief in their survival, namely that their faith has meaning to them. Because it has such a positive, formative effect in their lives, it ought to have meaning for others. On the one hand, that is a magnificent affirmation of the intimacy of God and Christ in our lives. God has come to us in particular places and ways. But it comes out as one of the subtlest forms of racial imperialism. Since God came to me my way, I'm sure he'll do the same for you. The Puritans came to this country to worship God in their own way—and make sure everybody else did the same. It is very hard to separate the intimate affirmation of God in particular cultural symbols from the objective, denominational statements about a universal faith.

Therefore congregations go through several stages or phases of transition. The first is to expand their base.

When the congregation feels that the community is changing, which means that some of the best families are moving out, the temptation is to become metropolitan. For some churches, this means to run and catch up with these families. "Let's move."

For others, it means this will no longer be a neighborhood church. "Let's be a regional congregation." There is a thrust to expand the program, or buy space for parking, or develop a whole new educational wing. Often the resources of a couple of generations are burned up in the process of trying to go metropolitan.

Tremendous burdens are placed on the staff. Everyone must do their thing right. The preacher should preach great sermons; the youth leader should be a pied piper. The pastor should call to the outermost ends of the suburbs. There is a tremendous temptation to do it bigger, better, and on a regional basis, which provides an umbrella for the quiet departure of some of the best families. Those with children assimilate into their new communities; those without keep coming back. And everybody keeps paying.

All this is an affirmation of confidence in what the congregation was. "We still do it this way, only now on a regional basis." Congregations can pull it off for a while if they have a location that is highly visible from some arterial highway, enough money, and leadership that attracts attention in one way or another. That is phase one. It often ends with a pop. The pastor leaves, the funds are expended, and the church collapses. I know of one church that made it that way. Almost all of the churches I studied had tried it, and all of them wanted to.

The second phase is one of contraction; the church squeezes down. Members admit that there is a change going on, and they become a covenant community.

They seek out a second layer of resident leadership, and agree that not many of us are left, but we can do it! They take the burden off the pastor and increase in all the statistics of commitment—attendance, money. It confuses the life out of those of us who are looking for a statistical change. There's a bump in the graph. What's even more fascinating to me is the strong affirmation of faith that is elicited in this second phase. The congregation admits to cultural change and reminds itself of its religious, rather than its cultural, roots.

On the other hand, there is a hands-off attitude toward the denomination: "We can do it ourselves, thank you." The denomination may contract with a congregation for a particular ministry, but otherwise they don't take aid from anybody. In the second phase the religious emphasis is vigorous, and the response is schizophrenic, even to the explosive reasons why people ultimately leave. After agreeing to stay, people explode for the oddest reasons—the pastor, his family, his management of the transition. In one case a marvelously successful fund drive was concluded without any coffee or refreshments. The chairman got mad and left the church. He couldn't deal with why he wanted to leave, so he exploded.

The theology behind this is, in H. Richard Niebuhr's terms, transformationist; it's a congregation that seeks to manage through Christ in its particular experience. I think such congregations can survive and be very effective. In fact this contractual relationship was the only bridge that seemed to change congregations racially in any numbers.

The next phase is an accommodation phase. It's when the church suddenly runs out of money. Then they are willing to work with anybody. It's a time when they realize how much human turmoil surrounds them, and they try to be a pastor to the changing community. They engage in a great many pastoral services, and will share whatever they have in order to get the resources to survive. They will loan the church to those who agree with them and rent it to everybody else who has money. They'll even rent the pastor—if you'll excuse the phrase—let him work for someone else in a spiritual capacity or even get a secular job in order to keep part of his time. They'll bring in some federal programs, bargaining with whatever they have for time to survive.

Sometimes, there is even a preparation for passing the baton. If the culture that is moving in is very different, they will permit another congregation to use the church. Of course, not at the hour when God is there. If the culture is Hispanic, there are some overtures toward working together. If it's Asian, the group is allowed to use the facilities without even participating on the church's boards. But if it is black, there is no such tolerance. Blacks speak English and must join our culture, our church. I don't know of a single black congregation that is sharing facilities with a white church in a changing community.

What eventually happens in the accommodation phase is that the younger congregation stays there just long enough to be pushed around a little, and then they are strong enough to go out and buy a place of their own before the old congregation gets around to selling their space to them. I know of only one church where a genuine passing of the baton took place.

The basic emotion in this phase is grief. We have been invaded! We are an occupied country. The congregation gets what it bargained for, time, but loses what it said it wanted, the transition of faith to a new group. Such congregations can survive for a long time and can provide useful services to changing communities.

The last phase is leaving, which often gets very awkward. Churches leave either violently by wrenching the people from sacred space or quietly as in retirement. We Protestants find it difficult to retire individually. But how we love to die with our boots on. No congregation will die without a mission statement. So congregations often go into a long, low-energy period of depression, like sleeping bears. They are fine unless you poke them, or they get hungry. It is a state of utter exhaustion that, like a black star, can consume all the energy anybody pumps into it and is still relatively unmoved. Still I marvel at their capacity to hold out. The power of that faith against all other agencies and cultural groups is amazing! I'd love to find a way to harness it in some constructive purpose.

Two congregations I know of went into retirement programs where they gave up Sunday, deciding they were too old for all that stuff, and switched to a Tuesday program. We'll use this space, they said, to celebrate, to enjoy who we are and what we've been. We'll sing a few hymns, have some games, do some handicraft, and bring in a few sandwiches. A church that had 10 members on Sunday now has 200 on Tuesday! The retirement ministry of affirming people in their older years brought out innumerable people in that transitional community.

This depressed state is essentially a low-energy way to survive for a long time over and against dominant denominations. It is a Christ-against-culture mentality. Theologically it is the reverse of the great American dream where, as Niebuhr describes it, the American religious experience flows from sect to church. What essentially takes place in a transitional community is the flow from church to sect, following essentially the same theological outlook.

In the first phase, then, there is an affirmation of the congregation's own culture. In the second, the desire to manage it; in the third, the desire to survive in crude tension; and finally a denial that it's there.

What I have described is essentially the syndrome of a patient facing terminal illness. In the first phase, there is extravagant denial: that's the expansion of program. In the second, pent-up and explosive emotion: high commitment or deep anger. Thirdly, there is bargaining for time: just a little bit more with whatever I have to offer. Finally there is long depression, low-energy survival. That's a pretty dismal picture. And yet, it is a strong affirmation of how much faith means to people who hang on to it.

And although there are congregations that transcend—that go through the second phase and become another kind of church, an ethnic, racial affirmation of the faith—the people in those congregations still face the roughness of living with a culture that is alien. After all, God did not make himself known to them through Spanish. And though it may be the same God, it doesn't feel the same. They will follow this cycle through the depression phase until they have recovered some new affirmation of faith in a new area or the old place renewed.

If the new congregation begins from the old, it will stay smaller for a longer period of time. Still it allows the larger denomination to have a vision that is not possible if they close and leave. But it is costly in terms of growth. The church can begin again stronger and sooner if it closes. The Methodists have a way of doing this: they have enough black congregations to move one in. But most of us do not have that luxury. Some of us have tried to steal minority leadership and paid the price of joining with those who do not see the world as we do. Not all bad, but sometimes very sticky. It does, it can, begin again.

We Protestants have precipitated the crisis of changing communities through our mission-minded churches. We've told churches that they ought to be aggressive, and the people that they ought to discipline their lives so God will bless them in success. It is the mission-minded and the task-oriented person and church that cannot tolerate the stability of a community and are constantly on the move.

There is another theology besides this. We could call it catholic, a theology of stability, which affirms the need for tradition, for sacred place. There is a theology of people, for time that begins, as one of my friends says, when I get there and lasts as long as I can remember it.

Lest you think that's an easy theology for Protestants, tell me a good Protestant word that means status quo. And yet I think we need to understand and affirm those congregations that stay and counsel stability in our dynamic economy, as well as those that urge our mobility.

This suggests a kind of cultural pluralism that is difficult for those who insist they are right. We need strategies of coalition with people who don't think exactly as we do—coalitions to find alternate styles for education and health, coalitions to deal with policies in housing, or police. We need to find coalitional strategies that go beyond what we ourselves can provide, and that includes a kind of political pluralism. I say that despite the fact that the congregations that survived were those who had a single-minded commitment to a faith that God had spoken to them, and through them, in a particular place.

Finally let me affirm that I'm not opposed to churches speaking in the culture, having one cultural background. But some churches ought to transcend culture. I think it is the denomination's responsibility to affirm transcendence. Most of our denominations give social programs. I'd like to see a few of them give visions, a vision of the different ways God can speak to people's lives—some of which are transcended, integrated churches.

Integration now exists in three places. Either in the upper-middle class where everybody who can buy a $100,000 home goes to church there. So the church says, "Look, we're integrated; we have three blacks." Or it takes place near institutions—a hospital or university that provides for diversity of employment. Finally integration does exist in the high-commitment church that goes in when others have left.

It's nice to have integration, but we know that not everybody can or will. We need the denominations so we see the wider vision, but we can also affirm the separate ways of different cultures. The denominations ought to provide the vision for us. And the individual congregations ought to fight them for the right to be who we are. There ought to be a workable tension between the two. It is the affirmation of our diversity that makes transition possible, not trying to find a middle ground. It's not the reduction of tension but the admission of tension and enjoying it in God, in Christ. That's what makes urban ministry possible.

Eight

ANTIDOTES TO VICTIM-BLAMING

David Claerbaut

MORE AND MORE URBAN MINISTERS are leaving their buildings and going out into the streets where the people are. They are becoming interested in social programs because they have found that people's temporal needs must be met in order to have a positive effect on them spiritually. In the research I have been doing, these are the ministers who seem most effective. But if the church is going to become involved in social programs, we must avoid the fallacies that have blinded many others. Blaming the victim is one of them, the Achilles' heel of many federal programs that are failing.

William Ryan, whose book, *Blaming the Victim*, first

David Claerbaut

Dr. Claerbaut is assistant professor of sociology and psychology at North Park College and lecturer at Loyola University. He is a member of the Board of Directors of the Cabrini-Green Legal Aid Clinic.

exposed this fallacy, feels that this tendency is universal. People who are trying to begin effective programs are often blinded by "a set of officially certified nonfacts and respected untruths" that distort their focus. They are unable to see the real cause of the social problem, because they are caught in the victimization process.

How does this process occur? A social problem is first defined—for instance, crime, poverty, or low educational achievement. But most definitions today begin with those who are the losers and explain how they are different from the rest of society. Then these differences are stipulated as the core of the problem.

Once this core is stipulated, we are ready for the big final step. A government agency, a community organization, or a church designs a humanitarian strategy to correct that difference—which might be OK if it really did, but it doesn't. (Remember that these persons and institutions often have good intentions. Many of us who attack social programming and strategy forget that most of these people care. They are allies. But if they get caught in victim blaming, they are probably going to do as much harm as good.)

The greatest fallacy is that the victim is always expected to change. We don't change our institutions, the way we run our classrooms, or how we arrest people, nor how we distribute power and resources in our society. No, we try to change the victim, to drag the poor fellow up to the standards of the middle class. We define him as something (not some person but some *thing*) that needs improvement and enrichment. Some of the most famous people in sociology and government, those who are considered tremendous humanitarians, were victim blamers and never realized it.

Here's a classic example used by Ryan. The problem is lead poisoning: kids are dying from eating chips of lead paint. In a flush of concern, some pharmaceutical company decides to take on the costs of designing, printing, and distributing signs that warn against eating paint chips. They go into a low-income area and distribute those signs in every building where this could conceivably occur. These people are genuinely concerned about this chemical reaction, and people applaud, "Well done, thou good and faithful servant."

But they forget that lead poisoning is not simply caused by eating paint chips. It is the end result of the entire American system of slum living, slum landlords, and ghettoization. It comes from people buying buildings and stuffing as many human bodies into them as possible. It comes from letting those buildings run down to the point of near demolition. It comes from not enforcing the laws that forbid using lead paint in residential dwellings.

So who are the real enemies? Not the kids or their parents who aren't warning them effectively, but the slum landlords and the city inspectors who take a bribe and walk past as the priest and Levite while people are dying. We don't attack them because if you get into slum landlording, you're starting to play on the turf of property. To the American middle class, property is more valued than life! In some municipalities, if a person invades your property, you can beat him, or even shoot him.

One of the most tragic parts of this cycle is that the mother of the dead child has not only lost her child but also begins to feel guilty that she did not warn the child, or was not there to prevent the child from eating the paint chips. She has been socialized into believing that it's her fault—a subtle, yet obvious example of blaming the victim.

If I were an urban pastor and didn't know about

victim-blaming, I might applaud the pharmaceutical company for distributing those signs. (I want somebody to care, and distributing those signs may help in some way.) But doing that only blinds us to the real problem.

This is why victim blaming has a double edge. Both the victim and the rest of society, the part that really cares about these problems, are victimized.

For instance, there are two approaches to the problem of low achievement. The dominant one is the victim-blaming view: low achievement is the result of apathy. Poor people supposedly don't care about achievement. Statistics prove that the best predictor of a child's achievement in school is his socioeconomic status; and from that we derive the notion of cultural deprivation, assuming that kids from poor areas are blighted, deprived and therefore can't learn as well.

Then we falsely conclude that the way to deal with low achievement is through enrichment—Head Start, Upward Bound. All of these programs are characterized by the same thing—taking the child and trying to make a middle-class organism out of him. We try to change his desultory attitude by taking him to the zoo, showing him where the museum is, and bringing him into the wonders and glories of middle-class society. Then he will achieve.

Literally millions of dollars have been washed down the national drain in enrichment attempts, sometimes called compensatory education. Notice compensatory, compensating for the deficiency of the student not the system.

A non-victim-blaming approach would be decentralization. Most urban school systems are centralized. In Chicago, very few of the rules are adhered to, but if they were, every classroom in the city would use the same textbooks.

This city-wide edict comes from downtown. Now why is that a problem? Because it assumes that someone in the main office knows what is best for children very, very far away from that locale. Education isn't going down into the streets—down to the people's level—as some urban ministers are.

Another problem with inner-city education is money. The difference between the per pupil expenditures in the city and in the suburbs is astronomical. White and black middle-class people are packing their bags and their kids and heading for the suburbs, because they know a different kind of educational experience can be found there—one that deals with the culture of the community, with the child as an individual, and with the goals of individual development. We don't see that in the cities.

Teachers' attitudes are another problem in the city. Their morale is low because they deal with the difficulties we are discussing every day. And the rapid turnover of teachers in city schools increases this dissatisfaction. For instance, if there is an opening in the Chicago school system, it must be posted in every building; then teachers apply to transfer there on the basis of seniority. Obviously, the openings in the fringes, or more economically stable areas, are filled immediately, which means teachers are constantly leaving the city schools. Each year new individuals are introduced to the life and experiences of people in poverty areas, and before they really understand them, they are gone. Such turnover also has a deadening effect on veteran, inner-city teachers who soon want to leave because their colleagues are always changing.

Worst of all, the community has no feeling of continuity. Most urban ministers, especially if they are white and working in a black area, soon realize that the

number one thing people are looking for is a commitment to stay. "Will you remain with us, or are you going
to be gone a year after your program has failed and
Sunday night services aren't well attended?"

Another social problem that is susceptible to victim
blaming is poverty. What's the dominant view? People
who are poor are literally drowning in the culture of
poverty. Their whole way of life reflects poverty, therefore their values are poverty related. Many people feel
this situation is hopeless unless one can change their
views—get them to save money, wash their clothes, not
have sex with anybody out of wedlock, and respect the
law.

A non-victim-blaming approach would include increasing the opportunities for employment in poverty
areas. The main thing that is missing in low-income
areas is stable jobs and job opportunities. Almost every
major department store, factory, and industry has left.
Businesses leave because the community's purchasing
power is gone, and industries exit because they aren't
strategically located to ship their goods.

There's also a problem of income maintenance. Just
about everyone, from Ronald Reagan to John Kenneth
Galbraith, agrees that the welfare system isn't working
well. We don't have an effective income-maintenance
method. But there is no way of maintaining income in
the absence of jobs, and we have not found another
method of making sure people have enough cash to live
on.

Unfortunately people in poverty areas depend on the
government rather than the government depending on
them. In the suburbs this isn't true. Government officials, either local or state, depend on serving the community, because if they don't, they're out. In the city,
people are dependent on the government for financial

maintenance and housing, which includes rats and roaches in numbers greater than people. Year after year the same tired, old political hacks get back into office by intimidation.

Or, on the national level, can you think of a congressman or senator who is mainly known as a champion of the poor? There are ecologists, abortionists, and liberationists, but not people who represent the poor.

Another social problem is crime. What's the dominant view? It occurs in the slums, so it must be due to the social conditions there, which warp the criminal's personality. Therefore the police role is to patrol these communities and try to ward off violence in these "high-crime areas."

But the highest crime area in any city is the business district. If we were to take a more non-victim-blaming approach, we would begin by identifying the three types of crime. First organized crime, which supplies drugs, prostitution, numbers games, and Mafia hits. More money is made by organized crime than the two other types combined. The second type is white-collar crime—from Watergate to city corruption. And the third is street crime, which tends to be violent but is low in terms of frequency and the amount of money involved. Compared to the other two types, street crime is relatively minor. Yet when people think of crime, they think of street crime.

"We've got to get tough on crime. We've got to make our city neighborhoods safe," the new police chief in Chicago said in a post election interview. The main crime, he felt, is in the streets. Not in the Loop. Not building inspectors being bribed, or political scandal, or people being threatened by city officials.

In America we talk about law and order. But one can almost forget law; it's not important. What is important is order. Think about the crimes that bring incarceration: crimes of order—drunk and disorderly, breach of peace. But if an industry located near Lake Michigan is dumping effluents into the lake and endangering the lives of 5.5 million people who depend on that water, a government official gives the owner ninety days to clean up the plant, and then a fine if he doesn't.

If you are a car manufacturer in Detroit, they'll give you until 1975 to come up with a pollution-free engine, and if you don't, they'll extend it until 1980. But if you're poor and you grab a woman's purse and there's twenty dollars in it, you'll not get ninety days to give it back. You'll go to jail tonight. You'll receive legal defense from a public defender, usually a lawyer who is handling fifty other cases that day. Either the judge will declare you guilty, or you'll plead guilty. And if you don't receive a lenient sentence, it will be because you live in a high-crime area, and the judge thinks you'll hang around with undesirables and get into trouble again. So you'll go to that great rehabilitation institution called prison, which is the number one educator of all criminals.

We also have victim blaming in urban ministry. For example, some urban churches have a tutoring program. That's sort of a victim-blaming phenomenon. Kids are taught to read who are not learning to read in the public schools. I'm not against such programs, but I am pleading for a greater awareness of the victim blaming in them. While a church is inaugurating a tutorial program, it might also try to influence the schools to be more effective, so tutoring programs won't be necessary.

While the church is helping people whose buildings are without heat, it might also find out who the slum landlords are and begin pressuring city inspectors to crack down on them. While the church is working to stop crime in the streets (and it ought to because some of its parishioners may be victims of rape or mugging), it might also give some thought to a legal aid clinic. Or find out about redlining in its community—banks that aren't extending loans because they consider the area a dead community. And it will be, if no one can get a mortgage to buy a home there. That's a crime, too. It's a crime committed by people with striped ties and turtlenecks and clipped fingernails who aren't supposed to be criminals at heart.

We say to criminals, "Hey, I want to make you more middle class so you can make it in this system," without realizing that the system might be wrong. Is something wrong with the system of distributing justice? Any Christian should be able to find a number of places where he or she has channels to redress some of the institutional problems in the community

The problem with urban ministry is that you help one victim, and there are still a hundred more lined up behind him, suffering from the same problem. Christ ministered one at a time, and I affirm that. But you're going to get a much greater sense of accomplishment if you can kill redlining in your community, or get accountability in a school, and stop the problem from recurring.

If people in your community are aware of your knowledge of institutional injustice, which is what they see—if you're more worried about whether they have a place to sleep than about who they sleep with—you're likely to have a much greater effect in evangelism.

1. William Ryan, *Blaming the Victim* p.xii.

Nine

CHURCHES AND ENERGY CONSERVATION

Dennis Bakke

VOLUMES HAVE BEEN WRITTEN about the current world energy situation. It is not the purpose of this chapter to add significantly to those discussions or to provide any substantial analysis of where we are or how we got there. When viewing energy from the perspective of the church, however, it is important to keep in mind a few salient facts.

First, the era of petroleum energy is ending. It is somewhat disconcerting to note that the lifetime of to-day's middle-aged person will likely span the entire petroleum era; if you are in your late thirties or early forties, the world's supply of oil simply will not last much longer than you do. It is clear that in a relatively

Dennis W. Bakke

Mr. Bakke is the director of the Western Hemisphere Operations of the Al Dir'lyyah Institute of Geneva, Switzerland, a philanthropic organization principally concerned with assisting lesser-developed countries with alternative energy technologies and policies.

short sixty or seventy years most of the world's stock of petroleum will have been consumed. Future historians thus may note that major oil usage was a peculiarity of the period roughly between 1930 and 2010.

In addition, energy costs have changed direction. Figure 1 illustrates that until recently, the real price of all forms of energy was declining steadily. That curve has turned upward in dramatic fashion. High energy prices are a fixture of the future and should figure into all long-term planning.

FIGURE 1

REAL PRICE OF ENERGY FROM 1950 TO PRESENT

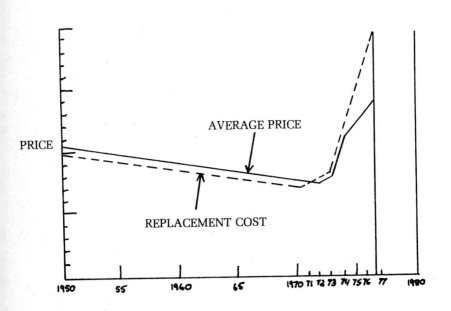

A third fact that ought to impress Christians especially is the unequal distribution of energy sources. Except for solar power, most of the known sources of energy exist within the Middle East, the United States, the Soviet Union, and a few other countries scattered around the world. Moreover, even though the United State's share of the world's energy supplies are significant, they are meager compared to its consumption. In the future, this will increase tension among peoples and nations and will intensify the problem of unmet physical needs in less endowed parts of the world.

Finally, the current rapid consumption of fossil fuels (oil and coal) poses considerable environmental concerns. These problems range from increasing amounts of sulfur and other toxic substances being spewed into the air, to increasing the atmospheric temperature at the earth's surface by massive burning of fossil fuels, to damaging agricultural and other lands through the extraction of energy fuels. Energy consumption has a major impact on our environment.

CHURCHES AND ENERGY

Why should churches be concerned about energy? What role does it play in the mission of the church? There are at least four answers:

Stewardship. As we face the closing years of the twentieth century, stewardship needs to be broadened beyond the traditional "time, talents, and tithes" to include energy. To be adequate stewards of energy resources, we must use them wisely.

We are stewards of God's creation as a whole and have been given "mastery" (Gen. 1: 28) over it. Certainly God did not intend us to despoil what he made good. We are responsible to use the world's resources in a way that benefits all mankind and at the same time keeps the earth habitable for future generations.

We need to reapply the message of the Sermon on the Mount, where Jesus told us not to worry about our lives and what we will eat and drink and wear, for God will care for us. Can we believe in such simplicity? Can we trust that God really has given us enough food, clothing, shelter, and even energy?

We can certainly believe it more easily than those in the Third World. And if we use less and at the same time learn to make better use of our resources, there can be hope for them as well. God requires our cooperation, our trust, our stewardship.

Global Justice. 1 John 3:17 says, "If a rich person sees his brother in need, yet closes his heart against his brother, how can he claim that he loves God?" (GNB).

We are undeniably "rich persons." Our nation is, in fact, the world's glutton, consuming commercial energy at six times the rate per capita of the rest of the world and several hundred times more than some developing countries. If all the world used commercial energy and other resources at the rate we do, all known reserves of petroleum, natural gas, tin, zinc, lead, copper, tungsten, gold and mercury would be used up within ten years. Oil supplies would last only six years.

The United States has 6 percent of the world's population, but uses 30 to 40 percent of the world's mineral and energy production. The huge Prudhoe Bay oil field in Alaska, developed at such incredible cost, would last only a year and a half if it were the country's only source of oil.

Altogether, the developed countries such as the United States, Germany, and Japan use 85 percent of the world's petroleum. No wonder, the Third World sees us as resource gluttons. This high energy consumption undermines the Christian message to the rest of the world. We must show our concern for others by reducing our use of scarce energy resources. Certainly, Christian churches need to take the lead in this mandate. Conservation of energy should be a prime concern for all church leaders.

Healing the Environment. The growing dependence of our country and the world upon nuclear energy creates unknown health hazards. A central issue of nuclear power is whether the radioactive materials can be kept away from all forms of life for generations. Even a small leak—say, 1 percent of the products of one plant—could contaminate hundreds of square miles for centuries. Can human beings create a system that will not allow even a minor failure? Can we continue to store nuclear wastes without releasing nuclear pollution into our water or air? Radiation, in the words of Senator Mike Gravel, is the "ultimate pollution." Yet, if we continue to increase our demand for energy at a rapid rate, nuclear plants and the incumbent risks will undoubtedly continue to proliferate.

Even more important may be the massive use of non-nuclear fossil fuels to provide us with electrical energy. Utility companies are now constructing the Southwest Power Complex, a series of five plants in Utah and New Mexico desert areas. One of these units will consume 50,000 tons of coal per day. When in full operation, the total complex will dump 600 tons of sulfur dioxide into the air per day (sulfur dioxide reacts with water to become sulfuric acid). The plants will produce 1,140 tons per day of nitrogen oxides. And there are other harmful chemicals produced by the burning of fossil fuel.

Not long ago the federal government announced that

research had led to the conclusion that 90 percent of cancer is caused by environmental factors. We have dirtied our world's air, water, and earth partly through our wanton and careless use of energy. It is time we used energy more wisely and looked for new, less polluting sources.

Church Energy Costs. The fourth major reason Christians and churches should save energy is their own pocketbooks. Table 1 taken from the Joint Strategy and Action Committee's 1977 survey shows the significant increase in energy costs among churches. Costs have doubled, tripled, and even quadrupled in certain cases since 1973. Predictions are that these costs will continue to spiral, rising from 10 percent to 20 percent per year over the foreseeable future.

TABLE 1

MEDIAN COST (DOLLARS) OF
FUEL/ENERGY PER DEGREE
DAY USED TO HEAT AND/OR
COOL 1,000 SQUARE FEET OF
CHURCH BUILDING

City	1970	1975	1976
Boston	$0.0200	$0.0355	$0.0393
Charleston	0.0531	0.0528	0.0955
Columbus	0.0180	0.0321	0.0325
Denver	0.0146	0.0202	0.0239
Houston	0.0343	0.0567	0.0753
Minneapolis	0.0177	0.0262	0.0293
Phoenix	0.0294	0.0527	0.0557
San Diego	0.0525	0.0861	0.0941
Seattle	0.0178	0.0301	0.0336

Tampa	0.0215	0.0428	0.0604
Average, all localities	0.0279	0.0435	0.0540

If you take time to calculate what these rates will mean over the next twenty years, the results are frightening. At an inflation rate of 10 percent per year, compounded yearly, the cost of the fuel will be 6.7 times what it is now after twenty years; at 15 percent, the cost would be 16 times; and at 20 percent inflation per year fuel costs in 20 years would be a staggering 38 times as much as today's cost.

We know that current energy costs are hurting many church budgets to the point where outreach programs to the community and the world are being curtailed, and in some cases the staff is being reduced and buildings are being abandoned. Saving energy to save money is important if we are to manage the resources God has given us to use for his purposes.

CHURCH ACTION

Stewardship, global justice, environment, and cost make action by churches on energy matters essential. What follows are practical local responses to this challenge by the church as an institution and, to a lesser extent, by church members. This does not mean that political activity and concern over energy policy are not important. Churches and their members should influence energy policy, but much needs to be accomplished in their own backyard.

THE CHURCH FACES PROBLEMS

Church Program. It is impossible to deal with energy until a church analyzes its mission, especially as it relates to the use of its buildings. What is the outreach mission strategy of the church? How important are church-owned buildings in that strategy? Once this integration is complete, a church can then evaluate possible changes in church programs that consume energy. Table 2 from the JSAC survey shows the types of changes some churches have made to conserve energy. Note that nearly half of the churches answering the survey had made no changes.

TABLE 2

CHANGES MADE IN CHURCH PROGRAM TO CONSERVE ENERGY

	Number of Congregations	Percent
No changes	104	42.3%
Used homes for some meetings/programs	56	23.2%
Consolidated meetings into fewer days/nights	53	22.0%
Consolidated meetings/classes into fewer rooms	46	19.1%
Moved worship service out of sanctuary	21	8.7%
Canceled some worship services	20	8.3%
Shared facilities with another congregation	10	4.1%
Other	18	7.5%

Table 3 breaks out these changes for urban versus nonurban churches.

TABLE 3

ENERGY-RELATED CHANGES IN
PROGRAM FOR CHURCHES IN
DIFFERENT SETTINGS

Type of Change	Percent of Churches Making Change		
	Urban	Suburban	Rural
Moved worship out of sanctuary	12.5%	5.5%	9.4%
Cancelled some worship services	7.9%	8.2%	12.5%
Consolidated meetings/classes into fewer rooms	28.4%	14.7%	15.6%
Consolidated meetings into fewer days/nights	29.5%	21.1%	6.3%
Used homes for some meetings/programs	23.9%	24.8%	18.8%
Shared facilities with another congregation	4.5%	3.7%	3.1%

These program changes may not be applicable to your church, and even if made they may not be sufficient from an energy use perspective. If the church program uses the building only once or twice a week, the church is making poor use of its capital assets. A seldom used building is extremely difficult if not impossible to make energy efficient at an economically acceptable cost. In these cases churches should search the community to find other uses for their buildings.

Operations. A second area of energy analysis in which every church needs to engage is the conservation of energy in the operation of its buildings. Initially this will probably require the creation of an energy study group or task force. Table 4 shows how few churches in some of the major denominations have formed such a group.

TABLE 4

CHURCHES WITH STUDY PROGRAMS ON ENERGY STEWARDSHIP

Denomination	Percent of churches
United Church of Christ	29.4%
American Lutheran Church	21.3%
United Methodist Church	18.9%
United Presbyterian Church U.S.A.	18.7%
Lutheran Church in America	11.8%
Southern Baptist Convention	10.3%
American Baptist Churches U.S.A.	9.5%

The mission of such a committee is first to look at the usage patterns of the building so eventual actions can be concentrated where they will do the most good. The group should then evaluate each possible option for using energy more efficiently. The analysis should start with the heating system and move to such things as lighting, thermostat setbacks, and even ceiling fans to drive down the warm air that rises to the top of high-arched sanctuaries. In addition, attention needs to be paid to insulation and air filtration. An excellent checklist for such an analysis is available from the American Baptist Extention Corporation in Valley Forge, Pennsylvania.

Finally, churches need to look at alternative sources of energy, especially solar, for their existing buildings. If a significant amount of hot water is consumed, for example, a solar water heater may be economical. If the building has an unobstructed south-facing masonry wall, it may be able to construct a simple Trombe wall to assist in heating the building. The diagram below illustrates how this technique works.

A PASSIVE SOLAR HEATING SYSTEM

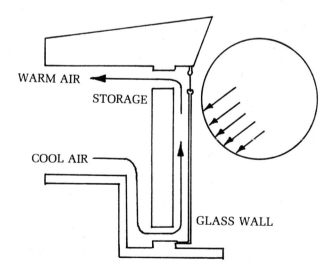

WARM AIR

STORAGE

COOL AIR

GLASS WALL

Solar greenhouses, especially in the city, are another option both to provide food and to supplement heat requirements. Other possibilities are available or will soon become available. These need to be reviewed by every church. Actions should be taken where the investment costs of such improvements can be recouped through energy savings and other benefits in future years.

New Buildings. The options for solar and other efficient designs are even more varied and economically feasible in new buildings. A congregation should look for an architect sensitive to energy considerations and demand that the building design, site location, orientation, and the heating/ventilation/cooling systems be appropriate.

Energy Stewardship of Church Members. We must not forget that individual members consume considerably more energy than does the church building or programs. In most cases, more energy is used to transport members to a single Sunday service than is consumed by church building operations for that entire day. Thus, it is important to urge parishioners to use public transportation, drive smaller cars, eat less energy-intensive foods, and choose recreational forms that require minimum amounts of energy.

CONCLUSION

Clearly, the need for energy conservation in churches is great. High costs, the theological command for stewardship, the requirement to aid the poor, and the impact on the environment all demand that we pay more attention to energy.

Each church should study its program's relationship to the use of its buildings to obtain better utilization. An energy committee should be formed in every church to study the energy usage pattern in its physical facilities, analyze potential conservation actions, and seek alternative energy sources. Finally, each member needs to review his or her use of energy and make appropriate adjustments to reduce consumption and use our God-given resources more wisely.

The tables in this chapter are reprinted from *JSAC Grapevine*, Vol. 9, No. 5, Dec., 1977.

Energy Conservation Manuals:

Energy Checklist for Churches, American Baptist Extension Corporation, Valley Forge, Pa. 1978.
In the Bank . . . or up the Chimney? HUD (Housing and Urban Development), Washington, D.C., April, 1975. Order from Superintendent of Documents, U.S. Government Printing Office, Washington, DC 20402 for $1.70.
Project Retro-Tech, teacher's kit for course on home weatherization, Federal Energy Administration, Washington, D.C., May, 1976.

General Construction and Weatherization Guides:

Insulation Manual—Homes/Apartments, NAHB Research Foundation, Rockville, Md., Sept., 1971.
"Common Sense Guide to Caulks and Caulking," *Popular Science*, Sept., 1974.
"Weatherstripping," *Consumer Reports*, Feb., 1977.
"Exterior Caulking Compounds," *Consumer Reports*, 1977 Buying Guide.

General Information and Heating Theory:

Other Homes and Garbage, Leckie, Masters, Whitehouse and Young; Sierra Club Books, San Francisco, Calif., 1975.
Mechanical and Electrical Equipment for Buildings, Fifth Edition, McGuiness and Stein; John Wiley and Sons, New York, N.Y., 1971.

Solar Energy Information:

The Solar Home Book, Anderson and Riordan; Cheshire Books, Harrisville, N.H., 1976.
Solar Energy: Fundamentals in Building Design, Anderson; McGraw-Hill, New York, N.Y., 1977.

The Fuel Savers: A Kit of Solar Ideas for Existing Homes, Scully, Prowler, Anderson and Mahone; Total Environmental Action, Harrisville, N.H., 1975.
Direct Use of the Sun's Energy, Daniels; Yale University Press, New Haven and London, 1964.

Economic and Governmental Information:

Retrofitting Existing Housing for Energy Conservation: an Economic Analysis, Peterson; U.S. Department of Commerce, Dec., 1974.
Energy Conservation in Nonresidential Buildings, Salter, Petruschell, and Wolf; NSF, The Rand Corporation, Oct., 1976.

Simpler and Energy Efficient Living

Simple Living, Ziegler; Brethren Press, Elgin, Ill., 1974.
99 Ways to a Simple Lifestyle, Center for Science in the Public Interest; Anchor Books, Garden City, N.Y., 1977.
350 Ways to Save Energy and Money, Spies, Konzo, and Calvin; Crown Publishers, New York, 1974.

Ten

URBAN FATIGUE

Dr. David I. Frenchak

A SIXTEEN-YEAR-OLD GIRL in an urban area was asked why she didn't go to church anymore; she had once been an every-Sunday attender. She replied by saying that four of her five pastors during her lifetime had suffered emotional breakdowns.

I know what she refers to. Before coming to my present position, I was a pastor in Boston for eight years. Only afterwards did I even realize my burned-out condition during the last eighteen months of my pastorate. I struggled on from day to day, but my reserves were simply gone.

What is burn-out? It is more than just being tired. It is more than just being discouraged. It is the snowballing

David I. Frenchak

Dr. Frenchak is the director of studies of the Seminary Consortium for Urban Pastoral Education, a combined program of academic studies and practical urban experience in cooperation with six midwestern evangelical seminaries.

effect of physical, emotional, psychological, and spiritual fatigue. A person who is physically tired but still has his wits about him can continue to cope. But when all the strengths have turned into weaknesses, one becomes incapacitated.

THE SYMPTOMS OF URBAN FATIGUE

Perhaps the most obvious psychological symptom is a negative attitude. The urban minister begins to view both his people and his coworkers with cynicism and even contempt; they become little more than objects of mission in his eyes.

Closely related to this is a detachment from people. He becomes impersonal, hard, cold; he begins to categorize people in his mind—for example, "the poor" or "the politicians"—even though they may not fit the stereotype at all. But he finds it easier to dismiss human beings if they have labels.

The victim of urban fatigue may also tend to intellectualize situations and problems. "That's the way it is," he may say about a particular injustice. "You can't do anything about it—that's just a part of living in the city." His emotional resources are spent; he can no longer get angry about things that deserve anger. Nothing can touch him; compassion is gone.

The physical symptoms run from just plain exhaustion to a variety of psychosomatic illnesses: insomnia, ulcers, migraine headaches, backaches. Sometimes the urban pastor or worker recognizes the source of his fatigue or illness, but often he does not.

Neither may he trace back the roots of his social symptoms: marital conflict, suicide attempts, and in some groups, alcoholism. These too can be indicators of urban fatigue.

THE CAUSES OF URBAN FATIGUE

Why do these kinds of human tragedy occur?

One primary cause is the *constant confrontation with failure.* We live in a success-oriented society. We get strokes for succeeding; we celebrate our successes; they make us feel good.

Anyone who has worked very long in the city knows that the occasions for celebration do not come along very often. We push for societal change—and the society doesn't seem to change. A visitor came to my city not long ago and said, "Chicago looks the same way it did five years ago. What have you Christians been doing?" He wasn't trying to be spiteful; he was just stating the facts.

The problems are simply massive. For every ten people you help, there are at least a thousand more who need help, and perhaps more desperately than the ten you helped.

And the ten you helped may be back with the same problems tomorrow. Your efforts didn't last very long. You thought you had them on the right track, and the next morning the telephone rings again.

This causes us pain as well as anger. We evangelicals don't like to own anger; we think it is bad and it needs to be repressed. Or if we do own our anger, we search for someone to blame it on. Soon we are deep into hostility and sometimes bitterness.

Meanwhile, we also feel guilty. A voice inside whispers, "Aren't you a child of God? Don't you have the power of the Holy Spirit? Why aren't you accomplishing any more than you are?"

Those who minister in the city are in great need of an adequate theology of failure. Evangelicals may not be able to come to terms with what that means, but if we are going to survive in the city, we must learn to deal with failure.

A second cause of fatigue is the *urgency* of our task. The faculty of SCUPE (Seminary Consortium for Urban Pastoral Education) meets for a retreat each year, and last year we included our wives. One of them, a professional woman in her own field, said later, "I've never been with a group of people who were so *intense,* so driven to do something *now.*" She finally had to leave the room. And later commented, "I couldn't take it anymore." Perhaps she had more sense than those of us who stayed.

Because we view the urban mission as so urgent, we sometimes do shabby work. We hurry projects along, and then when we look back, we feel less than proud of what we actually accomplished.

But at the same time, we are trapped by our messianic complex; we think we are the only ones who know how to do things. If someone offers to help us, we don't know how to utilize their skills. We can only suggest that they do their thing in another area. The person often flounders for lack of direction, while feeling cheated and unappreciated.

Perfectionism is a disease. It is very catching, and at the same time, it is almost undetectable to its victim. Nevertheless, it denies all Christian concepts of humanity and the sinful nature. We are not perfect; we cannot do perfect work; we are going to fall short sometimes; we need one another.

I have much to learn from my black brothers on this

score. They seem to be able to look at urban problems and still relax. They live in it, do what they can do, and keep their sanity. I tend to want to work twenty hours a day and get everything fixed *now, my way.*

That is not a healthy way to live when dealing with urban systems, which are impersonal, slow, and yet demanding. In the city, half-hour tasks have a way of taking a full day and eighteen phone calls. A city pastor will try to get some action on behalf of a parishioner or the community. Then after a day of wrangling with one bureaucrat after another, he comes home to face his wife's innocent question, "What did you do today?" He's not quite sure. Dealing with systems and institutions is not easy.

So we get angry and declare, "The system has got to change." That crusade can be even more exhausting. The danger is that we can become so intense at changing the system on behalf of people that we lose touch and stop communicating with the very people we are trying to help.

Another unfortunate cause of our fatigue is the constant confrontation with physical violence that is part of urban life. I serve on the board of a counseling center, and a very interesting thing happened at a recent board meeting. We were visiting informally before the meeting started, and every person around the table had a tale to tell of some recent act of violence against their person. The toll of such a life-style is undeniable. It produces fear as well as anger. Both of which are undeniably tiring.

Urban ministry demands a certain *style of work* that contributes to fatigue. Who keeps regular office hours in an urban parish? I remember trying to do so in Boston— it simply would not work. The city runs twenty-four hours a day, and so do most of its pastors. Work becomes unstructured, subject to the demands of the traffic, the telephone, the unexpected.

But apart from such external factors, burn-out is also caused by *loneliness and alienation*. Most of us can think of former friends who don't seem to come around anymore now that we're working in the city. They no longer understand our language, and we don't care to go back to theirs. Our lives have taken different routes. Even one's own family sometimes does not comprehend or support what we believe God has called us to do, and we must constantly justify and reexplain ourselves.

Urban pastors sometimes feel alienated from their own denominations, whose support of the urban ministry that bears their name is not always strong. Pastors can become disgruntled and feel that "they don't understand what needs to happen—they don't share the vision. Why am I still affiliated with this body, anyway?"

Meanwhile, we do not always find warm friends in the community. In terms of white vs. black or white vs. brown, rich vs. poor, powerful vs. powerless, suburban vs. urban, educated vs. poorly educated—we are often on the wrong sides. We are in a strange, new society that is opposite to our heritage, and although we argue for the oppressed, everyone knows we fit better with the oppressors. This, too, causes tension and the conflict that leads to urban fatigue.

NEEDED THEOLOGIES

Our difficulty with coping with such pressures reveals several gaps in our theology. As mentioned before, we badly need a theology of failure. We have not adequately wrestled with the reality that the symbol of

Christianity is the cross of Jesus Christ.

I am not sure that we know the full meaning of that symbol. More often, our symbols are the dollar sign or the aspirin. Christianity is founded upon the cross: sacrifice, dying, rejection, failure. Only on the far side of that failure do we come to glory and resurrection.

Secondly, we need a theology of power. We need to comprehend that all power—every bit—belongs to the Almighty. And he, in his wisdom, has chosen to share it with a lot of different people and systems.

Now whenever a number of people have power, there can be but one result: conflict. Our task is not to avoid conflict, but rather to use it for good. Urban ministry is more than being nice and making people happy all the time. It also involves relating to power structures, which God has ordained, and pursuing justice on behalf of the people to whom we minister.

A third theological necessity is a realistic view of sinfulness. We live in a sinful society and relate to sinful people. At the same time, *we* are sinful people. We too have a dark side, a shadow. City people are not going to be entirely good and pure as a result of our ministry, because we ourselves are not entirely good and pure. We need to face this.

NEEDED REMEDIES FOR URBAN FATIGUE

Here are four suggestions for persons in urban ministry who wish to avoid burn-out:

1. *Wake up before it is too late.* Pay attention to what is going on inside of you, and take steps to repair the damage.

2. *Find a support group.* You simply cannot go on

alone. You need one or more persons with whom you can share your burdens, your pain, your anger, your joy, your satisfaction, your frustration. You must find a place where you can speak freely.

If you cannot do this with your denominational colleagues, go outside to other brothers and sisters in the Body of Christ. It was this kind of support group that saved me from total exhaustion in Boston; I went into clinical pastoral education and found it extremely valuable. It was a regular meeting in which the others held me accountable and listened to me regarding every aspect of my being.

People often come to such groups with a tremendous amount of denial. They don't want to own up to being tired or weak; they keep smiling and saying everything is all right. The others in the group must gently let such a person know that they sense that things are not all right. If the person continues to deny it, confrontation may be necessary to get down to reality. But if the group cares deeply enough for one another, they will be willing to confront.

3. *Get adequate training.* Nothing is more exhausting than trying to do something you don't know how to do. The city offers a multitude of resources that can enable us to accomplish tasks in half the time—if we know where they are. Community organization, for example, requires certain kinds of skills, and there is no sense in trying to reinvent the approaches and strategies that have already been perfected by others.

4. *Learn how to minister to yourself and your own needs.*

On the thinking level, keep your mind alive through reading and education. On the feeling level, get involved with an interpersonal relationship that will not allow you to pretend or deny.

Take time for sensory stimulation—seeing, hearing, smelling. If you enjoy music, let the music do something for you.

Stimulate the intuition as well, by meditating and praying regularly. And don't forget the physical level, where exercise and vacations play a needed role. It is amazing how many urban people in ministry think they don't need a break. They have forgotten the truth of the statement, "Only lions love a martyr."

Urban fatigue is a real and present danger not commonly understood. But with adequate attention to theology and to our practical needs, we need not succumb.

Resources

"Burn-Out," *Human Behavior* (Sept., 1976).

"Stress," *The New York Times* (Nov. 20, 1977).

January, 1978, issue of *Periodical Studies in the Spirituality of Jesuits.*

"The Wilderness State" and "Heaviness Through Manifold Temptations," *John Wesley's Standard Sermons,* Vol. 2.

PART THREE
The Church
That Ministers

Eleven

THE MINISTERING CHURCH

William Leslie

I HADN'T BEEN ON THE URBAN SCENE as a pastor very long before I realized that as one person I wasn't even going to dent the urban problems. I saw that if anything were going to happen, it was going to be because we had learned to train and mobilize lay people. We had to get something going so that those who had leadership and enthusiasm would come and be a part of what was going on, and then others would get involved.

William Temple once described the church as "the only institution in society that exists to serve those who have not yet become its members." I think the average Christian would be a little shocked by that because today's Christian sees the church as an institution to

William H. Leslie

Dr. Leslie is pastor of the LaSalle Street Church, Chicago. Under his leadership, the church has grown to include the Near North Counseling Center, the Cabrini-Green Legal Aid Clinic, LaSalle Senior Center, LaSalle Street Young Life.

minister to himself and his or her family. Obviously, the church has to minister to its own peoples' needs. If it is to be a truly ministering church, however, it has to have a high priority on meeting needs and caring for people who are not yet and may never be in that institution.

Unfortunately, most churches today are more like clubs. People get together and pay a certain amount of money to see that certain privileges are extended to them and that their needs are met. They aren't interested in people outside the club membership. The church, on the other hand, is supposed to be a vehicle through which Christ can mediate his message and minister to needy people throughout the world.

We need to challenge the concept of the church as a private club taking care of its own on at least three grounds: first, the Bible doesn't present the church in this manner. We spend a lot of time arguing about inerrancy and a lot of other things when there's much plain biblical truth that we could be obeying and putting into practice.

Second, the needs of the city demand a total mobilization of believers. Most of the people we work with are not the kind with whom you can put in an hour a week and expect to see dramatic change in their lives. Instead, these are people with nine or ten problems: legal hassles, family or relational problems, someone in the family on drugs or alcohol, financial worries. Leading them to Jesus Christ and giving them a foundation of discipleship provides a place from which they can start to rebuild their lives, but it takes a lot of people with a lot of different kinds of knowledge and skills to meet all those needs.

Thirdly, a lot of people have turned off Christianity and Jesus Christ because of their experience with the institutional church. They don't even consider becoming a disciple of Jesus Christ an option because of what they see of the people of God. We need some radical renewal within our churches, and part of that will come as we really start to care for other people as the early church did.

So for these, and many other reasons, we need to help the church once again become a ministering church. Now, how can we turn a church around? The typical church is like the situation in professional athletics. Twenty or thirty thousand people go to the game, pay their money, sit in the stands, boo and cheer, and eat popcorn—and watch about twenty people play the game. The crowd comes to be entertained and amused.

We've done the same thing in church. On Sunday mornings, our buildings are full of gifted people (and people with latent gifts) who at most are taking up the offering or maybe teaching in the Sunday school. Now both of those jobs are important, but that's not all a church ought to be offering her people in the way of challenges.

We have professionalized the church. We hire a few staff members to do all the significant ministry. And the lay people pay their money and sit out there to boo and cheer. And that puts a lot of pressure on the minister because he knows he's being compared with the minister down the street. When a pulpit committee comes by to look you over, they ask you three questions: How much has the attendance increased while you've been here? What has happened to your offerings? And have you built any new buildings? In order to be successful, according to the world's criteria, we have to perform in those areas. But when I stand before God, he isn't going to ask me about numbers, or offerings, or buildings. That's all peripheral to God. I think God is going to ask what happened in the lives of the people I touched.

I've had to wrestle with these competing value systems, and I decided that I would encourage our church members to become active, rather than passive, members. To do that we all needed to understand our roles and our expectations of the other person's role, and we had to communicate with each other about what we were doing and what we thought the other persons involved were doing.

The lay person who sees the church as a place to rest usually wants to leave the Sunday service with some good feelings (and certain lay people have to be chastened in order to feel good). He really sees himself as the fan at the baseball game who pays his money so he can boo and cheer. And it is the minister's job, in his mind, to hit a home run every week. I try to remind my congregation that the best hitters only hit three out of ten. If the church can give me that kind of average on my sermons, I'll be glad to play on this team any day.

The church and I had to do a lot of talking about how I saw my role, which I defined as player/coach. Then we had to change their perceptions of themselves, until they saw themselves as *active* people. Our church happens to come from a strong biblical, evangelical tradition, and I realized that the only way they were going to change was if I could first show them a model from the Bible. I knew that if I could develop the theology from the Bible, then all I would have to do, over a period of two or three years, would be to stand up and keep calling for obedience. Eventually it would come, if I did it in a nice way.

It's so important to initiate change with love and compassion. Jim Wallis, from *Sojourners* magazine, and I were talking recently about how we had changed over the years. He said that one of the major things in his heart and mind was reconciliation. He had been struck by the story in Scripture of Jesus and the rich young ruler. Jesus told the man he had to sell all his goods and give the money to the poor. And Jim said that he had been going around the country telling people they ought to sell all they had and give it to the poor, but he had been overlooking what else the story said: "Then Jesus beholding him loved him" (Mark 10:21). We have to love people, not berate them.

So one of the first things I did was to search out biblical principles that would help to bring about the sort of change we were looking for in our church. These are some of those principles that helped us.

First, the fact that the Kingdom is present, although its consummation is future. God reigns and rules in the present; he is Lord over people's lives who now acknowledge him as Savior. That doesn't mean any of us are perfect. I think we're all on the way, and he accepts us where we are—which gives us a real lift in accepting others where they are. We all have a responsibility to extend the reign of Jesus Christ in people's lives in our present society.

Paul, in both Colossians and Galatians, talks about being delivered from this present evil age. He says that this age is under the dominion of the principalities and powers. Right now we are locked in a struggle with those principalities and powers who run this age to win back lost turf for Jesus Christ. Sometimes that turf is people's lives, sometimes it is an institution of society.

Recently the reading level of some high-school seniors was tested, and the scores averaged third grade, second level. Someone needs to say to the power structure that God is displeased by this sort of thing. Parents are going to have to act differently, teachers are going to have to act differently, and we're going to have to work for a different administration. People's lives are being affected, and it is our job to see that God's will is done in that school, as well as in our church.

Our church staff includes two attorneys, because we have found that in most urban legal systems there are two standards of justice: some call it a white and a black justice; I call it middle-class and poor justice. We have to monitor these institutions in Jesus' name.

We also have to nurture them, picking up the good things that are happening and expressing our appreciation for a job well done. We have to celebrate with them the little gains so that the people within the system do not get discouraged.

Our mission is an extension of Jesus' mission. That involves leading people to Jesus Christ, but it also demands that we be involved in the society around us as salt and light.

The second principle is that of servanthood. We know of at least three times when the disciples had a conversation about who was the greatest. The last time was on their way to the supper in the upper room—the night Jesus was betrayed. The reason nobody had washed anybody else's feet was that they all wanted to be the greatest, not the least. But Jesus told them that the principle of the Kingdom is the direct opposite of what they saw in the world. Out there, the one who is the greatest has the most people serving him. But he who is greatest in the Kingdom of God, Jesus said, is the one who serves the most people. He gave us our model when he said that he "came not to be ministered unto, but to minister" (Matt. 20:28). We would avoid a lot of hurt feelings in the church if we came to give rather than to get.

Now the servanthood model, of course, must be carefully balanced with other scriptural truths. We all need to know that we are not only to be servants to each other, but that we *are somebody*. Those people in the congregation with inferiority feelings need to have their self-esteem built up, and we need to be sure both messages are preached and shared. But we must not lose sight of the servanthood model, in which we learn to give ourselves away.

The third principle is that the church is the Body of Christ. In Acts 1:1, Luke mentions all that Jesus *began* to do and to teach. The emphasis in the Book of Acts is that Jesus is still doing and teaching, but now he's working through his people. Just as Jesus was at one time incarnate in the world in a physical body, so now he is incarnate in this world in his Body, which is the church. We are his hands, his feet, his mouth, his people.

A friend of mine went every day to a high school football practice, even though he was not the coach and had no children on the team. When I asked him why he did that, he said, "Jesus Christ lives in me. When I go to that football practice, Jesus Christ is present in a way he wouldn't be if I were not there. He has a lot more options because I am there."

One part of Christ's work, the atonement, we can't help with—that's a finished work. But Christ also had a message and a ministry, and we need to share the one and perform the other. In evangelical churches, we have tended to share the message, but not perform the ministry. We are supposed to be doing what he did while he was here—caring for people.

Generally speaking, the church likes to think that if it can keep coming up with new programs, then everything will be all right. As Keith Miller and I were talking about how to change the church without coming up with any programs, we decided to try an experiment. We would suggest changing everybody's life-style to one of caring. We were leading a meeting of about a thousand people. We asked all the people who were present at that meeting to list the actions of either a church or a person that most affected or changed their lives.

When those thousand people told about the experiences that changed their lives, there was not one program mentioned. Instead, they said things like "someone called me up one night and invited me over for coffee," "somebody touched me," "a neighbor brought over a hot loaf of bread." We don't need a lot of new programs with budgets. All we have to do is to tell our people to care for other people.

The fourth principle is found in Ephesians 4:11-12, which says that God gave the church pastors and teachers "to equip the saints for the work of ministry" (RSV). It doesn't say that the pastors and teachers were going to do the job for the rest of the church. Elton Trueblood said, "We gave the laymen the Bible in the sixteenth century; let's give them the ministry in the twentieth century."

Another principle is that of taking on the incarnational stance. Jesus didn't opt out of difficult situations. If he didn't want to get involved in human situations, he could have stayed in heaven. But he stepped out of the ivory palaces and came down here where we were, and he got beat up. People got whips and beat him. Eventually he was nailed to a cross. Isn't he calling us to this same kind of incarnational love? It really bothers me to see Christians living in air-conditioned barracks fly air-conditioned planes to drop gospel bombs down on people and be back home in time for the early evening television shows.

It helps to present to the church some worthy models to look at. I think of the Church of the Savior in Washington, D.C.; the Church of the Redeemer and West Memorial Baptist Church in Houston, Texas; Fairfield Baptist

Church in Chicago; and the First Presbyterian Church in Berkeley, California, just to cite a few examples.

We had a book-of-the-quarter program going at our church, where people would read about various ministries and begin to become acquainted with what other churches were doing. They could then apply the relevant parts of those ministries to our own situation. At the same time, we developed the means for a few people at a time to reach out into our community in meaningful ways. Our staff acted as enablers, as a clearinghouse for skills and concerns.

My other personal strategy is to come to a church with the understanding that I am making a long-time commitment to that congregation. We cannot bring about meaningful change in a church in a year or two without tearing the body apart. My goal is to slowly build into all the people in the church these fundamental principles, even though that may mean moving more slowly than sometimes I like. That way, if anything should happen to me, the basic commitment to be a ministering church will still be there.

As a player/coach, my goal is to get everybody on the field. As a few people caught on to that concept, they got excited and involved. Then more began to get the idea. And slowly we are becoming a ministering church.

Twelve

VIABILITY OF ALTERNATE URBAN LIFE-STYLES

Tom Finger

ONE OF THE MOST SIGNIFICANT surprises on the religious scene in the 1970s has been the resurgence of evangelical Christianity. And an important surprise within the surprise has been the strengthening of the social consciousness among evangelicals. Evangelicalism has usually stressed the contrast between Christian existence and that of the surrounding world. For many Evangelicals, Christian life begins with a distinctive conversion, involving a radical break with one's former way of life. The life-style of the convert is expected to differ markedly from that of others. Evangelicals have often regarded with skepticism those individuals and

Thomas Finger

Dr. Finger is presently combining his teaching at Northern Baptist Theological Seminary with an interim pastorate at Circle Church, Chicago. He is a faculty member of the Seminary Consortium for Urban Pastoral Education.

institutions who make no thorough-going Christian confession. They belonged, it was assumed, to a realm of darkness soon to be judged for its evil.

However, anyone concerned with those who suffer under the evils plaguing the urban world—poverty, racism, crime, and the rest—soon realizes that these problems have inescapable and intertwining structural dimensions. For example, many people are poor because so few jobs are available in their area. The job market has dried up because businesses have left the area. Those businesses have left because the majority of people are too poor to support the business. One can do little to alleviate this problem without addressing the need for jobs. That immediately lands one in the complex of economic and related political issues. But if, as evangelicals have often held, the economic and political realms stand under God's judgment and are rapidly heading toward destruction, how does the gospel apply? Would not evangelical theology be a poor foundation for significant social concern and involvement? In other words, evangelicals have stressed the difference between personal experience and the life-style of the rest of the world, whereas involvement in urban affairs means dealing with structural and systemic issues that affect everybody.

Some evangelical Christians are now finding a theological perspective with which to deal with these problems. First, evangelicals have always claimed that Scripture is their final authority. In recent decades, largely through the stimulus of the civil rights and antiwar movements, it has become painfully obvious to many evangelicals that the Bible speaks repeatedly about God's concern for justice for the poor and disadvantaged. Second, not only have evangelicals in general moved cautiously toward social involvement, but some of the most radical and best-known urban experiments in alternative life-styles claim an evangelical heritage.

As a result, conservative Christians are asking if there is a biblical way of combining the traditional evangelical concern for distinctiveness of Christian conversion and life-style with an emphasis on those social problems that are inevitably related to more systemic realities. Or, on the other hand, are efforts like alternative urban Christian communities really based on more liberal, humanitarian, or radical leftist philosophies? Are they perhaps just passing fads, or at least out of joint with traditional evangelical theology?

To try to find answers to these questions, we will look briefly at a theological basis for communal life-style and urban involvement and then see to what extent that theology is expressed in three alternative Christian communities: the Sojourners, Jubilee, and Austin Community Fellowships.

A BIBLICAL THEOLOGY OF THE KINGDOM

In the Old Testament, the Kingdom of God is understood in two senses. First, and less frequently, it refers to God's sovereignty over all the creation. For instance, "the Lord has established his throne in the heavens, and his kingdom rules over all" (Ps. 103:19, RSV). Throughout the Old Testament, however, it is clear that though God may ultimately rule all things, he is seldom acknowledged as king. Consequently in the second, and more familiar usage, the Kingdom of God refers to a people called out from among the nations to live under God's rule in a special way. The first usage of the term *Kingdom* emphasizes that God's rule extends to all dimensions of created existence, including its economic, social, and political aspects. The second shows that God's foremost method of actualizing this rule is to focus his presence and power through a particular people called out from among the rest. God told Israel "You have seen what I did to the Egyptians, and how I bore you on eagles' wings and brought you to myself. Now therefore, if you will obey my voice and keep my covenant, you shall be my own possession among all peoples, for all the earth is mine, and you shall be to me a kingdom of priests and a holy nation" (Exod. 19:4-6).

How was Israel to be a priest to mediate God's reality to the rest of the world? In large part, through keeping God's commandments, many of which regulated social life. Moses explained that God's laws "will be your wisdom and your understanding in the sight of the peoples, who, when they hear all these statutes will say, 'Surely this great nation is a wise and understanding people.' . . . What great nation is there that has statutes and ordinances so righteous as all this law?" (Deut. 4:6, 8). In other words, God intended his nature to be revealed largely through a nation whose corporate life was marked by justice, fairness, and concern for one another.

Numerous passages in Exodus, Leviticus, and Deuteronomy spell out this social structure. The powerful and rich were limited in what they could do or acquire. Those who could most easily be deprived of social and economic benefits, such as the orphans, the sojourner, and the widow, were carefully protected. These principles are perhaps best summarized in the directions covering the year of the jubilee (Leviticus 25). Every fifty years, all debts were to be canceled, all slaves freed, and all land sold for debt restored.

In the course of Israel's history, however, the nation as

a whole tended to turn away from God. The prophets repeatedly denounced the breaking of God's social laws and restated God's concern for widows, orphans, and sojourners. God's special people, those living obediently under his Kingdom rule, became a smaller remnant within the nation. Still practicing God's justice amidst an unjust society, they frequently suffered and were, or became, identified with the poor and the needy. Many passages in Isaiah and Psalms use the terms *poor* and *needy* in a special way for God's people (for instance, Isa. 3:14-15; 25:4; 26:3-6; Ps. 35:10; 37:14; 71:12-14).

Though the number of the faithful remnant decreased, though the heart of God's Kingdom work was focused through an increasingly smaller and usually suffering group, the universal scope of God's redemptive design was painted in ever broader and more breath-taking colors as Old Testament history progressed. The renovation of the entire cosmos and even the abolition of death itself were glimpsed on the edge of the horizon.

Jesus began his ministry with the proclamation "The time is fulfilled, and the kingdom of God is at hand; repent, and believe in the gospel" (Mark 1:15). The Kingdom Jesus proclaims is clearly that of God's universal reign over all aspects of created existence. It is entered, however, only by those who make a radical personal commitment. They must be willing to give up all—their families, friends, social ties, and possessions—to attain it.

As opposition to Jesus grew, and his following dwindled, a small remnant of Israel still held firm at the core of God's plan. This remnant was to live by standards quite different from those of the surrounding world, as we see in Matthew 18—20. Humility, rather than pride, reigns (Matt. 18:1-4), and forgiveness triumphs over vengeance (Matt. 18:27-32). Weaker, less important people, even children are honored (Matt. 18:5-14; 19:13-15). Women's rights are increased over against men's (Matt. 19:3-10). Single persons have places of importance (Matt. 19:11-12). Most citizens of the Kingdom are poor or have become poor for Jesus' sake, while the rich enter with greatest difficulty (Matt. 19:23-30).

After Jesus' resurrection, the term *Kingdom of God* is less used, but the concept is central to the apostolic message. That's very clear from Acts (see, for instance, the summary statements in Acts 1:3; 8:12; 19:8; 20:25; and 28:23, 31).

In the New Testament outside the Gospels, Christians are sometimes called "heirs of the kingdom," indicating that the fullness of God's rule over all spheres of reality is yet to come. At the same time, however, God's Kingdom is powerfully, though only partially, present among Christians (Rom. 14:17; 1 Cor. 4:20; Col. 1:13; Heb. 12:28). It is both a present and, in some sense, a future reality. The Kingdom is present in small groups called out from the surrounding world. They are scattered, often persecuted, and unimpressive by worldly standards. Yet in language reminiscent of God's words to Israel, these Christian communities were "a chosen race, a royal priesthood, a holy nation, God's own people, that you may declare the wonderful deeds of him who called you out of darkness into his marvelous light" (1 Pet. 2:9).

The word *Kingdom* is heard frequently in the three communities we're examining. These fellowships are convinced, as evangelicals have always been, that Christ calls one to a decisive commitment that distinguishes one from the surrounding world. Being "born again" or "having a personal relationship with Christ" are meaningful phrases to most if not all within the communities, but their commitment is to something broader than personal salvation. It is a commitment to God's Kingdom, which is most dynamically present in groups of called-out Christians responding to the Kingdom. Such a corporate life, which is marked by strong concerns for justice and relief from oppression, will inevitably make an impact on those structures that mold social existence. These communities, then, express one way in which decisive personal commitment to Christ, seen as a call to Christ's Kingdom, inevitably influences the systemic or structural dimensions of life. When we are called to turn radically from our past and the ways of the world to Christ, that call is not simply to personal deliverance from evil; it is also a call to participate in God's Kingdom work. If that Kingdom work is understood as something God is doing throughout all dimensions of existence, then that call to decisive personal commitment and salvation inevitably flows into a life-style that influences the structures and systems around it. We can see, then, that a theology of the Kingdom provides a link between the personal and the structural tensions of living as Christians in the real world.

ATTEMPTS TO LIVE OUT THE KINGDOM

Now, let's see how this theology is expressed in some Christian communities.[1] Sojourners Fellowship is perhaps the best known of the three because of the journal that its members put out. It's located in the Columbia Heights area of northwest Washington, D. C. This area, which is almost totally black, was burned in the 1968 riots. Boarded-up and burned-out houses and

141

vacant lots abound, although the population is extremely dense and housing is very expensive. Only a few family businesses and small groceries have started since the riots.

Sojourners Fellowship is composed of about forty-five adults and eight children. There are no uniform regulations regarding membership, although there used to be. About ten individuals live nearby and relate closely, or intentionally, to the community. That is, they're thinking about joining eventually. About fifty others are less involved but participate in some of the fellowships' life and ministry. Sojourners functions as a church with the usual worship, educational, and pastoral functions. Its closest religious ties are with a larger international grouping of communities, the Community of Communities. Locally, Sojourners has ties with religious groups of similar socio-economic perspective including the Community of Creative Nonviolence and two communities of the Church of the Savior, the Day Community and the Community of Hope. They also participate in groups concerned about nuclear disarmament, military policy, and human rights.

Some members of the Jubilee Fellowship also put out a magazine, called *The Other Side*. They live in a working-class neighborhood of Germantown, Pennsylvania, which is approximately half black and half white. The neighborhood is somewhat stabilized; however, local stores are in trouble. The local schools are almost all black, and young white professionals are beginning to move in. There are strong community organizations, and the neighborhood is fairly safe.

Jubilee Fellowship has twenty-five adult members, six of whom are in the final stages of exploring the group, and eighteen children. Jubilee has a five-page membership liturgy that expresses the commitments of members of the group. A debate continues over the degree to which this statement functions as a statement of faith. That is, is it something official that says what you do if you're part of the community, or is it a liturgical expression that isn't binding in that sense? They expect a basic theological orthodoxy, a commitment to justice, a simple life-style, and an openness to challenge from other brethren. Like Sojourners, Jubilee fellowship is also a church. They belong to the Philadelphia Mennonite Council, they hold frequent services with the local Episcopal Church, and they may soon join the Community of Communities. They are active in several national groups like Evangelicals for Social Action; they have ties to Germantown community organizations and the Philadelphia Coalition of Human Rights.

Austin Community Fellowship is located on the very western edge of Chicago. Because of redlining and blockbusting, this area has changed racially from about 95 percent white to 95 percent black since 1970. Upwardly mobile and middle-class blacks are getting many of the large old houses into shape. But many other residents in the area inhabit crowded, crumbling apartment buildings. Only a few stores survive, and crime is a constant, though not overwhelming, problem.

Austin Community Fellowship has defined its membership more tightly than Sojourners or Jubilee and presently counts twelve adult members and seven children, along with five intentional neighbors and three of their children who relate closely. Unlike Sojourners and Jubilee, however, ACF is part of a larger church, the Circle Evangelical Free Church, which has about two hundred active members. About thirty Circle people who live in Austin or in neighboring suburban Oak Park are involved in various outreach ministries. For example, the Circle Community Center houses various youth

143

programs, a legal clinic, a family counseling center, and a health clinic. Each of the latter three is headed by a former ACF member, while the head of the center still belongs to ACF. ACF is thus the original inspiration behind most ministries in the area. Harmonious working relationships indicate that many former members are still within a larger undefined ACF orbit. In addition, individuals from other churches than Circle are being drawn to Austin Community Fellowship, and ACF is presently considering making its membership requirements a bit more flexible.

ACF has close ties with Reba Place Fellowship in Evanston and is, with Reba, part of a larger grouping of communities. The Circle Community Center has received government grants to work with various city and federal programs, such as hiring teenagers in the summer and counseling at local schools. Circle people have been involved in many neighborhood groups, but such groups have often been spasmodic.

These three groups operate, at least implicitly, from a Kingdom theology that combines the personal and structural dimensions of Christian faith. The strongest critics of these fellowships are those who strongly emphasize one dimension or the other and who doubt that these communities do justice to that one dimension. Many evangelicals wonder whether such groups do successful evangelism and cultivate the personal spiritual life. Jubilee Fellowship has had little success with evangelism, if that is understood as appealing for a personal decision for Christ. Similarly, the Circle Community Center struggles with finding out what evangelism should be and how it should be done. However, calling one to faith in Christ is seen by these groups as closely tied to an overall commitment and life-style; consequently measuring the success of evangelism by the number of decisions, or by specifying the particular time or place of decision, may be perhaps an inappropriate method. Many lives do seem to be reached and changed, but counting specific decisions for Christ may give few clues as to what's really happening. All three groups report that spiritual growth among their people is great, largely because of the deep commitment of their lives to one another. Jubilee and Sojourners acknowledge continual tension between their constant busyness and their need for personal prayer and corporate sharing. The membership of Austin Community Fellowship devotes more time to personal prayer and corporate sharing but has felt uneasy about how these relate to broader structural involvement.

More liberal or secular activists might wonder whether these groups' emphasis on a high commitment to a distinct Kingdom community doesn't lead to withdrawal from, or at least ineffectiveness in relation to, systemic or structural issues. In other words, isn't this Kingdom life-style pretty much a withdrawal from the world at large? How broadly effective are their approaches in relating to structural issues?

In answering that, one first needs to be aware that the theological perspective of such groups puts the question of effectiveness in a particular light. If the Kingdom often comes through the activity and suffering of a tiny remnant, then normal criteria of effectiveness have little relevance. Further, if such a group is often, in Jubilee's words, "a feeble light in the darkness of principalities and powers," one may seldom see exactly how its efforts are relevant to God's larger Kingdom work. Instead, one is content with trying to be obedient to Christ's call without adopting a specific urban strategy with precise and measurable goals. Yet with these reminders, something can still be said about the systemic effectiveness of these groups that have opted for a community life-style.

First, all three have attracted a fairly homogeneous group. Almost all are white. (All Jubilee and ACF members are white. Sojourners has one black family and a few interracial marriages.) Most of the members are in their late twenties or early thirties, come from middle-class, suburban, or rural backgrounds, and are fairly or very well educated. This homogeneity among members creates problems in relating to blacks, the elderly, the lower classes, and the uneducated—precisely the people they want to relate to. All groups say it is difficult to get across that class barrier.

In general, however, the effort of building community and deepening personal relationships has not hindered active community involvement. Sojourners reports that its simpler life-style and sharing of economic resources has enabled about 3/4 of the working adults to be involved with community and neighborhood projects that provide no or only a subsistence income. Chief among them are a day-care center, a food co-op, and hospitality for the homeless. With a possible exception of ACF, distinguished from the Circle neighborhood programs, the communities seem amazingly involved. Jubilee Fellowship has been successful in facing structural issues of Germantown and, to a lesser extent, Philadelphia. Members have participated in numerous effective community organizations. Jubilee has bought about a dozen HUD homes and rehabilitated them. They have been a significant force in stabilizing a potentially declining neighborhood. The Circle outreach programs have been successful in helping individuals through medical, counseling, legal, and youth programs. The number of neighborhood clients (as opposed to white suburban clients) has steadily risen in all these programs. These relationships are mostly, however, on a helper-to-helped basis. Circle's Austin people are far from effectively touching the large structural issues in the neighborhood. Finally, it should be noted that Sojourners and Jubilee, through their magazines and the speaking engagements that grow out of them, have given incalculable inspiration for many similar efforts nationwide. This effectiveness may well arise because their publications are not grounded in theory alone but in groups seeking to live out what they proclaim.

1. The data for these communities was compiled May 1978.

Thirteen

RADICAL ETHICS

John Porter

WE HAVE SEEN IN OUR DAY the rapid growth of alternative faiths. We have to ask ourselves what these sects and secular faiths have to offer our young people and in what ways they are challenging traditional Christianity.

In general, when we look back to New Testament Christianity, we discover that it was simple and radical. The early Christians were not encumbered with a lot of doctrine, although they had a doctrinal stand. Their understanding of the message and meaning of Jesus' death and resurrection was simple and radical: demands were made of the new convert to change his or her life in order to become a part of the fellowship. They had to give up living with several wives, they had to

John R. Porter

Dr. Porter is national director of urban affairs for Young Life and was associated with the late Dr. Martin Luther King, Jr., and with the freedom movements of the South and Chicago.

stop cheating, they had to clean up their lives.

Many of today's alternative faiths make similar strict demands on their converts. Usually those new in the movement have to spend a year or two in some risk-taking evangelism, often in a foreign country.

Those groups demand a strict and simple discipline on the part of their new members, or else the initiates cannot be a part of the fellowship or live in the community.

Communism is perhaps the fastest growing secular faith in the world, and it has a very simple and radical methodology. It includes a strict, often secretive adherence to rules and a powerful mythology that promises that one day this group will rule society. The members are then sent out to infiltrate groups already established in society—including church groups—and to move into positions of leadership in those groups.

These new eastern religions that are attracting so many of our young people today offer at least six things that hold their recruits. First, they offer human friendship. Many of our churches are filled with lonely, idle, bored young men and women, people who are dying on the vine. These faiths offer them simple, honest friendship.

Secondly, they offer a direct, immediate spiritual experience. Many of our churches fail to provide the youth with clear, simple steps in the faith. Often our doctrine and rules get in the way. If a young convert ever came to one of the board meetings, or a session meeting, he would be scared away from the church, because he would have heard the same thing he hears all the time in the secular world.

Thirdly, these groups offer dependable authority. Many of us Christians fail to demonstrate that we really believe in Christ and Christian authority. We're timid.

We don't want to offend anyone, and so we applaud a person's individualism when they go out and do their own thing. These groups, on the other hand, are able to say, "These are the rules you must follow if you want to be a part of our community. You have to wash the dishes. You have to go out and sell the flowers."

Fourthly, these alternative faiths offer a simple, natural way into believing without getting lost along the way in complicated doctrine, rules, and meetings.

Fifthly, they offer many, particularly females, an opportunity to get away from an overwhelming domination of males in our society. Now I'm not a women's libber, I believe in a society in which men lead, but not one in which women are dominated.

And finally, these groups offer a clearly stated concern for health, ecology, and conservation—God's creations.

These six very simple elements are radical in the sense that they cause the new member to feel that he or she can enter and within a short time can understand why he or she is there. Now that's radical.

In addition to these alternative religions and secular faiths, we could point to a growing hedonism, narcissism, the beauty cult, a spiraling divorce and separation rate, the gay movement, child abuse, and suicide rates that all call for radical responses from Christians. All denominations are saying that they have a growing shortage of clergymen. Young men and women are saying they do not feel called; they say the problems of serving others is too much for them.

Historically, a great deal of our seminary and secular education does not tend to produce graduates who are able to lead congregations, because those young people have not begun to live themselves. They need years of maturity, of experience. Theorizing about life has its place, but it's not a substitute for actually living through a separation or divorce, adjustment to a job and career, and moving from place to place in order to find work. Sometimes it takes five, ten, fifteen years to get your bearings in a relationship. Most of our Christian graduates are not matured as speakers, preachers, teachers, evangelists, counselors, or organizers. How does a young man, just out of seminary, counsel someone who has been married and has several children? He may draw on the theory he picked up from a class in pastoral counseling. But the theory without the experience is one-sided.

Many of the young men and women we turn out are culturally snobbish, and we have trained them to be that way. They are too intellectual, too cerebral to communicate complex theological terminology to just plain folks. They want to talk about hermeneutics, and we ask, "Herman who?"

It took me three years after I graduated from seminary to learn to communicate with my congregation. I wondered why the guy down the street who hadn't gone to seminary had ten times as many people in his church. I had the methods, the programs, the systems. That preacher had 600 members. He had learned the folk art of communicating the Word of God in simple, what I call radical, ways with boldness, with confidence, with a sense of authority, and with the knowledge that he had been called to minister to that neighborhood.

A lot of our young people are not convicted or converted at a deep enough level. A lot of them are not even sure that Jesus is Savior and Lord of their lives. A lot of them are afraid to go out on the streets and talk to somebody else about Jesus because it is both embarrassing and frightening. Their doubts will show and that person they are talking to will not be convinced.

How do we overcome the problems of immaturity and insecurity in our Christian leaders? In order to sustain what it means to be a part of the body of Christ, we need to break with that part of the individual call that turns a man or a woman into a lone-ranger Christian. Every Christian, leader and layman, needs to be surrounded by several persons with whom, if not daily, then at least once a week, we spend at least a couple of hours.

In that time together, the first order of business would be to get into God's word and tarry there. Then pray together, lifting each other up spiritually, and allow both anxieties and gifts to flow into that corporate body. In that group, there's no leader—all are equals before God and each other.

That sort of group makes radical demands on every member. You are accountable to the other members. You don't miss a meeting because you want to go to a movie or because you are tired. These groups are an attempt to get back to the simple, radical life-style the disciples had. That radical commitment was what enabled them to turn things upside down, and that's what we need in our Christian communities today.

What we don't need is more sophisticated theology. We're already at the saturation point theologically. We know so much that even Jesus would be hard put to impart a fresh theological thought to us. But what we do need is to start obeying what we already know. We need to humble ourselves and submit to God's authority.

Then and only then will our lives be consistent with our words—and our influence as salt in the world be as salty as Christ demands.

Fourteen

THE GIFTED
URBAN LAY PERSON

Michael Roschke

THE FANTASTIC BOOK *Alice in Wonderland* provides a good analogy of lay ministry in the church. The March Hare is concerned because his watch has stopped, so he shakes it, opens it up, and then dashes in some butter to see if that will help it start ticking again. It doesn't work. The Mad Hatter comments wisely, "I told you butter wouldn't help it."

"But it was the best grade butter," replied the March Hare. Like the March Hare, the church has tried to accomplish worthy goals by using the wrong resources. That, in a sentence, is possibly the biggest handicap facing effective urban ministry.

But before we can even talk about using the right

E. Michael Roschke

Mr. Roschke is currently a missionary in Chicago's Uptown community. Begun by Roschke in 1971, this ministry now includes three full-time ministers, two teachers working in a community-based learning center, three counselors, and ten community workers.

resources, the gifted urban lay people, we must understand the climate the urban church finds itself in. We must understand how the mental health professionals, the medical profession, social workers, law enforcement officers, politicians, and teachers relate to the poor. We must also sensitize the urban lay person to find his or her own worth and dignity; they must realize that they are gifted by God's Spirit and are a people of promise. Too many of our urban lay people are now only on the receiving end of someone else's care. More need to be equipped to be givers. How can we do that?

First of all, the church in the city, like the church anywhere else, tends to have its lines of accountability and authority established with a definite pecking order. We choose ministers on the basis of competence, leadership skills, organizing abilities, and their backgrounds in theology, psychology, and sociological training. Then these folk are supposed to go where the people are and try to prepare them to be in ministry, to show them the way. Well, that isn't all bad—these ministers are well trained. But it creates a we/they syndrome. We train folks *up here* in our various professions in the urban church, then send them to help folks *down there*. Although it's subtle, that we/they syndrome begins to say to urban lay people, "You're a little less on the ministry totem pole than I am." There's a built-in tendency toward theological rhetoric and cultural isolation and aloofness in too much cloistered training.

For example, when I first came to Uptown, a poor white community in Chicago, I had to literally learn a new language from my street-wise friends. I was never taught this in seminary, because I wasn't going to a different language group, or so I was led to believe. But we were wrong. The people in Uptown speak a totally different language than I knew. I had to be at their level. I had to understand what they were saying. People told me they were going to go eat dinner at the *sally*. That was the Salvation Army. People told me that they had their *green cards* so they could get into a clinic—which meant their medical card from the state. People talked about *hanging paper*—that's forging false checks. People talked about *panhandling*—that's when somebody comes up to another person and says, "Hey buddy, you got twenty-five cents for coffee?" And a good panhandler in Uptown can get as much as thirty dollars in an hour of work on the streets. I had to let all those words become a part of who I was before I could articulate the gospel to those people in a way they could hear it.

Our church culture, despite its intellectualizing of why people are down and out, for too long has had this subtle prejudice that the pastor is over and above those who are being served. That thinking is not only true in terms of the minister, it applies to the other professionals in the community as well. We see the have-nots as those without as good an education, or without as much wealth, or without as much power to control their lives, or without as much responsibility, and therefore less than we are. No, the gospel says that Christ has made each individual a special person of God. With their personality and with their God-entrenched gifts, they have the ability to meet the needs of many, many people. It's hard for the urban minister and the urban church to allow the urban poor person to lead, to take full responsibility for programs, and to fill full-time staff positions. The congregation or the ministry must be alert to the problem of the inner city and the struggles of the people to survive, but the direction always seems to be called by the professionals.

The church and the clergy often prevent lay ministry

from happening for a number of reasons. First, the pastors need a system and need to be needed. That overrides the willingness to equip the urban lay person. Where will I fit in if all these people do these other things? Who will use me? The pastor has a fear of being dispensable. We've been trained in seminary to *do*, not to *enable*. Scripture, on the other hand, gives us models for equipping, being a catalyst or an advocate, standing with people until they can stand alone.

Another trap is that leaders in the church, especially the pastor, can set themselves up as the head of a pyramid structure. The image is that of the pastor at the top of the organizational chart. Then come the staff members, the boards, and councils. Finally there is the majority of the congregation—individuals who are gifted, but whose gifts don't fit into the slots already set up by the church. How can these people make use of their gifts if the church structure ignores them?

The third problem comes when the people of the congregation act as if the pastor were the hired Christian of the community. And with a professional Christian around, the rest of the congregation feels that they can relax.

Another problem is that most churches have no forum to see how a core Christian community can begin to develop. Seldom is a time and place provided where people excited about the gospel can gather for prayer and the inner journey. Where in the typical church program does that fit? We can learn from our black brothers and sisters how that can happen in a worship service. We can also learn from our Quaker friends who don't do anything until they first sit for half an hour praying and listening to what God is saying.

Finally, we perpetrate generalizations or myths when the leaders in the church say, "Well, we'd just love to be a more active church, but the people just aren't there yet." We say the urban people are too sick, too disabled, or they're on welfare. What's that got to do with having a gift from God? We assume that anyone on welfare can't be responsible enough to carry on mission and ministry in the church.

So for all these reasons it is extremely difficult for the church to allow or enable or permit or equip people to use their gifts. Then a stalemate occurs between leaders and the people of God, and the church becomes only a delivery system—"You've got a hurt; we'll deliver the remedy."

These problems and others have molded the lay people until the urban poor are content to come to church services and merely sit. They are unaware of their gifts, and they must be taught that they have something to offer. It is our responsibility to go back to these people that we've ignored for years and to say, "You're gifted. You're special." And then help them learn to express their gifts.

It is not only in the church that we disavow people's ability to be in ministry. Oftentimes in the mental health profession, psychologists and other professionals relate to the urban lay person as someone with problems, as a person with not much to give. The person who comes into a mental health center for counseling is called a client, a person who is coming to get some service from the pro. We live in a society of experts whose function is to dispense their knowledge to the people who need help.

Granted, much caring happens in the mental health field as well as in the church. Granted there is some expertise there to get people back to life. But to get them back to do what?

For example, here's senile Aunt Sally sitting in the

nursing home. If the only thing we think Aunt Sally can do is to receive our care, she will live up to our expectations. But my conviction is that God doesn't just leave old people around who are senile. No, she has a purpose to fulfill. I sent a welfare mom who had three kids and was always depressed to sit at Aunt Sally's feet one afternoon a week. Even though her stories were a bit repetitive, you wouldn't believe what Aunt Sally began to do with that welfare mom. She began to share things like caring for plants, and the next week they had an hour session talking about how when you have green things around it gives new life to you. The point is that God needed her to help this other human being.

One day I came home from work and shared with my family at the supper table that I was rather depressed because a man who was suffering from alcoholism and who had been living outside for about three months with no roof over his head seemed to me to be hopeless. During dinner, my daughter Melissa said (now here's why God has need of urban young kids—she's only three), "Dad, why don't we pray for Ray?" I had not only not thought of it, but even then I didn't pray for him at the supper table. That night when I sat down with her to read a Bible story and talk before she went to bed, again she said, "Let's pray for Ray."

The next morning I started to walk down the alley on my way to the office. The first person I see walking towards me is Ray, drunk already by 9 o'clock. I said, "By the way, Ray, I'd pretty much given up on you, but my daughter Melissa, hasn't. She prayed for you last night. She cares for you." He stumbled onto a bus, went out to a mental hospital, and got himself into an alcoholic treatment program. Ever since then he has been sober, and he distributes food out of our community pantry to the hungry. Melissa never gave up on who he was—she was the gifted lay person who could pray. Her caring for him changed his life.

We need to begin to have the eyes of faith. What does that mean? I'll tell you how God brought this across to me personally.

A couple of years ago I found out I was going blind because the cornea of my eyes were deteriorating. Eventually I found I could get cornea transplants, so I probably won't go blind if it's God's will, but he didn't let me find this doctor for a full year. So I was wrestling with the fact that here I am an energetic minister in the city and I might not be able to see. What he was teaching me was that I was not supposed to see with twenty-twenty vision but with my heart. Christ said the eyes of faith look through the behavior of individuals to the person God made. That's what we are to enhance and affirm so that person can blossom. We need the eyes of faith to relook at people and to see the unseen. We need discernment. That means that when we see evil in the disguise of good, we call it for what it is. We can see hope amid apparent failure. Eyes of faith will help us discern that if people have given up on themselves, there is another way, there is more possibility than they've given themselves credit for.

A biblical illustration is from Mark 8. That's one of my favorite miracle stories. Jesus comes up to the blind man, touches his eyeballs, and says, "Can you see?" The man says, "I can see people, but they look like trees walking around." So then Jesus touches his eyeballs a second time, and then the man says, "Now I can see clearly." That's what the church needs—a second touch from Jesus Christ. Sometimes we need a hundredth touch to begin to see people again.

When we truly see people, we want to enable them to use their gifts. How do we do that? First we have to help

159

the person with whatever his felt need is, holistically. If he is hungry, we help him get food. If he needs a job, we help him get a job. We are not telling him he is less of a person than we are, but we are enabling him to have wholeness.

Then, we need to let a relationship develop between the helper and the helpee, and to let those tags dissipate, so that God's people are beginning to reciprocate in ministry to one another. Sometimes that takes a long time to happen.

The third step is to get the person who came for help involved in a Christian caring community. Our goal is not that they come to worship, although that's good too, but that they meet with other Christians to study God's word, pray together, and share their struggles.

At that point we begin to equip that person to identify his gift, his strength from God, his ability. That takes listening, discernment, and relationship. Once we've enabled the lay person to see his gift, we have to discover the specific needs within the community and then match the gift with the needs.

Four years ago, I met a man named Ken who was living in a parked car. You can't get too much further down and out than that. He had cirrhosis of the liver, black lung disease from working in a coal mine in West Virginia, a cataract in one eye, and ulcers. His needs were pretty obvious: how were we going to keep him alive? My wife made homemade chicken soup. We got children from our learning center to take him sandwiches during the day—a lot of things like that. I would go to the car and sit in the back seat, and he'd sit in the front, and we would pray together. I took him the Lord's Supper and counseled with him, but nothing changed in his life for about a year.

Then one day while I was visiting a school some of the

children asked me what they could do to help people. As a result, the children of this one school began to write him letters, draw him pictures, and pray for him everyday. Some of them put his name on the refrigerator door at home so everytime they passed it, they'd see it. They started mailing all these things in to me at my office. Why did they have to send them to me? Because living in a parked car, Ken didn't even have a mailbox. I had to get Christians from our caring community who would daily take a letter or a picture to him in the car. And they did this. Unbelievable as it may seem, the impact on him was phenomenal. One day he came in and tore all those letters up in front of me and threw them on my desk. He called me the worst names in the book, and then he started to cry. He said, "It doesn't follow."

I said, "That's the good news. It doesn't follow that Christ would care for me but he did, and he does. And it doesn't follow that these little whippersnappers in Mt. Prospect would begin to care for you, even though they never even met you. But God first loved them so that they in turn can reach out and love you."

He then got into a treatment hospital and the relationship was still cultivated. Some of these kids had their parents bring them to the hospital where he was. Of course they weren't allowed to go up in his room; they were kept in the lobby, and he had to be wheeled down in a wheelchair. Then they could tell him that they were caring for him.

When he came back, it was a year before we asked him what he could do. We plugged him into our worship services and our Bible study groups. Then, finally, one day I took him out to lunch and said, "Ken, what can you do? What would you like to do as a gift that is within you from God to meet the needs of other people?"

I didn't know what he could do, but I still asked him

that anyway. He thought about it, and then he said, "First of all, you preached last Sunday on the prodigal son story where the man goes and leaves his father, and then he falls down and eats with the pigs and comes back. That helped me see that I have to make some relationships right. I'm going to go to all these people in my family that I've ripped off."

That's what he did. He went to those people and started mending the relationships that he had ripped apart. Then he came back to Chicago and said, "You know what I'm going to do? I want to start some stores for you—used furniture stores, a clothing store where we could let people have some decent clothing that could be given out with dignity."

And I started to think. Who could better manage some stores than Ken? He was the one who had been in the alleys. He was the one who had lived in parked cars. He was the one who knew the street people. So we got him stores. We opened up two stores, and you should have seen him blossom. Oh, not in flashy ways, but as a gifted urban person.

A group of mentally retarded people passed the store every day as they walked from the workshop to where they lived. He started inviting some of them to come in. One man had the problem of having an enlarged head, and he couldn't even reach down to tie his shoes. Ken gave him a new pair of slip-on shoes. Another old lady drifted over, one of the city's lonely wanderers. He gave her a new coat. He began to have those eyes of faith because he was really gifted.

That's not a success story; he's still got problems, even though he's been sober for four years. But he was enabled by the church to match his gifts up with the needs of other human beings. That's what we have to begin to do in the city so that people can begin to be the church.

In order for that to happen, we have to become so close with the people we're caring for that we allow them to care for us. Then we can understand their gifts and let them come forth. It's only when I'm vulnerable as a leader, when I share my weaknesses, that other people's abilities will come forth, because they'll know that they don't have to be some kind of phony leader.

The urban gifted lay person can also have a lot to give to the suburban and rural person. I shared with a suburban women's group once, and I asked if any of them would like to write some urban women who feel depressed and down on themselves and have actually given up believing that God could care for them. Some of them did start to write letters.

One afternoon an urban lady who was always depressed brings this letter in. She always felt that she was nobody. The suburban woman had written her a four-page letter. The last paragraph went something like this: "Oh, by the way, I'm writing this letter to you on a kidney dialysis machine. I can only do three things on this machine. I can pray, write letters, and sleep. But I wanted you to know that I care for you." That was the one part—that suburban woman really began to care for the urban woman. She thought that was it, until one day the inner-city woman took two buses and a train, and went out to visit the suburban woman. She told her what she knew about God's grace and that she wanted to care for her. She asked if she could make supper one day a week for her family, because the lady on the kidney machine had four children. That's the reciprocal nature of the urban person with the suburban person as they create a relationship in which caring can go back and forth. God enables both of them to grow. And that mutual ministry is, after all, the reason God wants pastors to equip the saints—even urban lay people saints.

163

Fifteen

THE URBAN CHURCH REVITALIZATION PROCESS

Raymond Bakke

IF WE ARE TO BE INVOLVED in the revitalization of the urban church, we have to do some homework. We need to study the community to which we have been sent, and we need to study the people who are there. We must understand each other's histories and develop a big picture into which our work fits.

To demonstrate this principle, we will look at a brief historical sketch of Chicago. The principles, however, as well as many of the specifics, could apply to any city.

Chicago was a city built where the rivers met the railhead. The Erie canal opened in 1825; the Ohio Michigan canal opened in 1831; Chicago was founded in 1831 and incorporated in 1833. This series of events was

Raymond J. Bakke
Dr. Bakke is the pastor of Fairview Avenue Baptist Church in Chicago. Dr. Bakke's church is in a Spanish neighborhood, and the congregation is a heterogeneous mix of seven ethnic groups.

not an accident. Illinois was settling from the bottom up, south to north; Alton, Illinois, was rivaling St. Louis as the largest city in the Midwest, and then the canal brought the Great Lakes' traffic into this part of the country.

About the same time, railroads and steam started to work, and Chicago remained up until the 1830s a Protestant village of migrants. At the time of the Civil War, there were close to fifty thousand people in the area. But then the role of the city began to change. Chicago, along with many northern cities, became a staging area for the industrial revolution. Chicago to the south had cheap fuel (coal), to the north, cheap ore. The only other thing needed to make Chicago work was cheap labor. That came because Europe was convulsing with revolutions.

The Irish potato famine hit in 1837, and the rural, Catholic Irish started to come in droves. Many settled in Chicago and worked in the stockyards on the South Side.

1848 was the year of the professor's parliament in Germany. Democracy failed, and Germany had a revolution and then began to prussianize. A lot of Germans came here and settled along Elston and Lincoln Avenue on the North Side.

Poland was undergoing struggles against Germans, and many others as well were caught up in this Slavic vs. Teutonic convulsion in Eastern Europe. Poland, unlike Ireland or Italy, for example, had a nationalism, a history, and Catholicism. When the Poles settled in the city, Chicago was the largest Polish city in the world. It is now the second largest city—larger than Krakow, smaller than Warsaw.

The Italians, meanwhile, started to experience trouble because Italy was divided between the northern states, which were expapal states, and the southern Sicilian sections. Italy was largely a patchwork of small-town Catholicism. When the Italians came, they settled on the West Side. These immigrant communities settled along the river, so the city was largely a Protestant front and an ethnic mix along the rivers. These immigrants came, viewing Chicago and the United States as the saviors of the world.

The industrial revolution had begun in Europe, and so, unlike most Americans and Scandanavians, who were largely rural in their orientation, many of these new immigrants had already lived in cities. When they came and settled along the river, they built the area to look like the place they left. The day Humboldt Park was built, it looked old. They brought their cultural heritage with them, and the church integrated that culture.

They became then Chicago's cheap labor, and the combination of fuel, ore, and labor together produced a unique city, an international city. Cincinnati, Detroit, New York, and other northern cities tended to have this same mix.

Up until World War II, the system worked. It generally produced a rising economy and a growth market. Cities became centers for manufacturing.

Then people started coming from the South, especially after World War I. Blacks slowly started to trickle to the North. Mexicans were brought by the railroad to be scab or cheap labor. Chicago was also still receiving second-generation Jewish and Polish immigrants from New York. The city was pretty much intact, and it was working. The ghettos were not prisons, but rather places these groups incubated. Nobody felt terribly oppressed in his or her ethnic groups.

By the fifties and sixties, these groups started to leave the city. They were more affluent and were heading out into suburbs to get a piece of the better life. They left a vacuum in housing and unskilled labor needs where they had been.

Meanwhile, Appalachia was plunged into poverty because the deep coal mines were being shut down. When the private enterprise system that produced cheap coal started costing too much, the companies pulled out. If they couldn't go to surface mining (they were already buying into oil and other investments), they just abandoned the territory. With TVA and in programs in the sixties, the federal government stepped in and picked up the whole enterprise. It took me a while to understand that my hillbilly friends had been on aid since the Civil War, because the public-aid case load is really just picking up the private aid case load that the companies had been responsible for. That's the backside of American capitalism.

The idea was to produce cheap goods in the northern cities. But when the cheap labor market ran out, and when a fuel source shifted, it was necessary to get new labor. The people who had been working in the deep mines or in the rural farms in the south, then began to come north to replace the cheap labor force. The migrants moved into the neighborhoods vacated by the upwardly mobile European immigrants.

Even Chicago, with its history of ethnicity, could not absorb all these people. Mississippi was the chief exporter of poor blacks. Alabama was the chief exporter of poor whites. The only kind of bussing that George Wallace never opposed was putting the poor on Greyhounds and shipping them to the North. In 1972, 49 percent of the Illinois welfare case load was from Mississippi, according to Senator Stevenson.

We gain another historical perspective when we remember that for the first one hundred years or so, our nation went west, largely to farms. That whole migration shaped our frontier, our theology, our hymnbook. We have a heritage of revivalism, sawdust trail camps, "work for the night is coming," and blue laws. But in the second hundred years, more Americans have moved north to cities than went west to farms. That's part of what is making our cities convulse.

Another dynamic that makes for tension involves the attitude of the people coming to the city. The immigrants of one hundred years ago came without many skills but with trust in the United States to provide for them. They viewed this as the promised land. They were happy to be here, even though they were poor. Their expectations were realistic.

The people who have come to the cities in the last twenty-five years for the most part are not immigrants, they are migrants. They are citizens—Puerto Ricans are citizens, Mississippians are citizens. They come here with implicit *distrust* in the American system. And they come at precisely the wrong time. The jobs are few. Where are coal miners going to dig in our town, and what are the rural Mississippi cotton pickers going to pick in the streets of Chicago?

They come and they feel like the door is closed. The former immigrants don't understand the new migrants at all, and the migrants don't understand the people who came from immigrant stock. The two groups have different histories.

The churches were started primarily by the immigrants, but the community is now largely occupied by the migrants. We have a situation of tension because of a lack of shared history and a lack of understanding.

One of the first tasks of pastoral leadership, then, is to study the community and the people who are there in order to appreciate their histories. Part of our problem as pastors is that we want to affirm a piece of turf—the church is *right here*. We were trained in seminary to have a geographical agenda that says, *"This* is where we concentrate." We need to realize that, in fact, we're in a migrant stream. In an Appalachian family, the one who really makes the decisions, might be down in Kentucky. That means if you're going to effectively pastor the part of that family in your city, you have to get access to that clan structure.

I have spent time in Appalachia learning about coal and cotton. In one year, I buried three people in the countryside outside Memphis. When we have a funeral in Tennessee, people come from Detroit that I don't see except at funerals. When the families get together, they rent a motel, and that's where I can minister to that migrant stream. I have learned that I am a pastor not so much to individuals as to families, clans. Rather than trying to organize these families around church agenda, we try to organize the church around the family agendas.

For my pastoral responsibilities, I have studied the hillbillies, the Hispanics, the blacks, and others. I'm now trying to learn Polish history. I've also studied the difference between Italian, Polish, and Irish Catholicism and the roles of pastors in those ethnic traditions. The Irish Catholics organized their urban churches after small town and rural models in Ireland. The Italians came largely from single towns in patchwork Italy, and they organized their churches in Chicago on small-town, godfather, extended-family models. Polish Catholics had a nationalism and a whole different style in Chicago; they were homogenous. For reasons unique to their European history and geography, the Irish built links to the Croatians and Magyars and other groups and ended up running Chicago. They had a political style that said, "Let's take over and work out in the community." The Polish, on the other hand, said, "Let's take care of our own." They built their own schools and gigantic cathedrals. Yet they had far more people here than any other group.

A second area we need to study is local church history. New members in our church knew nothing of the Swedish immigrants, so a few years ago, the class of older women created a history room. Their Sunday school classroom is now full of Swedish pictures of the old days. We try to take new members in there occasionally and imagine with them what it must have been like to be a Swedish immigrant in Chicago. We tell them the stories about how the people prayed on that location and gave an entire week's income—$273.02 was what the whole congregation earned in one week—to buy property. Some of those stories need to be retold. We can use history.

Pastors in urban settings should not be critical of the past, thinking previous generations never did anything right. We need to go back and try to get inside and understand the history of the church, master it, be the expert. Instead of saying, "We're announcing a program that this church has never done before," we should say, "Back in 1901, this congregation had faith to do thus and so, and finally we're going to try it again." When we can point to a precedent and affirm the history, that's not only political, it's biblical—that's what the prophets did when they kept saying, "Remember back then in the wilderness?" Keep that history alive, use it—it's important in the bridging of the migrant and immigrant groups.

We also have to be sensitive to the leadership patterns in the church. When I came to my church there were eleven leaders. Nine of them lived out of the city and the two that lived in the city did not live in the immediate area. The youngest of the eleven was fifty-four years old. The middle class and the middle aged had moved. I could not afford, financially or otherwise, to alienate that group. Those people were feeling bad because all of their own children had grown up and had gone to other churches. The parents had hung on a whole extra generation. They had enormous faith, commitment, and loyalty. They viewed me as their child because I was the age of many of their children. I understood that. I had to sense what that meant. I was coming to them, trying to tell them what to do because I had a couple of degrees and all this experience and vision and so on. But they were seeing me as a child substitute. My four immediate predecessors had been student pastors. Their agenda had been to come and get a couple years of experience and then leave. And of course the congregation paid them enough to guarantee that that would happen. And these people said to me, "Oh, you'll come and write a book, and then you'll leave too." Which is one reason I've never written a book. I don't want to use those people; that's already been done to them.

I spent an evening with each of these folks and asked them three kinds of questions. The first one was, how did you come to know Christ? Tell me about your experience. Secondly, I asked them how they came to this church. I wanted to share my faith with them, so they'd know we had a common faith. Otherwise, I might have appeared quite radical. I wanted to hear their personal history in this church.

Then thirdly, I asked, "If you could snap your fingers or wave a wand, is there anything you would like to see happen in this church? You've been here forty years; is there any unfinished business; do you have any dreams left?" I wanted to see if they could project any future. Several said, "No, we've got three to five years, pastor;

time is closing in. If we can just keep the Sunday school going and keep the youth group—that's what's important." The commitment was running fairly low. On the way home from those interviews, I taped my responses and reactions into a tape recorder and then typed that script. As I read and thought about our conversations I had some idea how far those folk could be stretched and what kind of commitment I had to make to those eleven people.

I figured it would take at least five years to arrest some pathologies, so I was making commitments five years down the road. I knew of the eleven people, six would be retiring and probably moving away within the next five years. I asked God for one man per year to replace those five, and I concentrated on family systems. As I look at a person, I try to see that I have a contract to work with a family. My goal is that the next generation yet unborn will have a Christian memory.

When I first came to Fairfield Baptist Church, I tried to get very involved in the community. I found that I was by myself because for nine out of the eleven core members, that was not their agenda. I was embarrassed to hear a parent from the school closest to our church say, "Oh, you're the pastor of the church where everybody lives in the suburbs." That was kind of humiliating. I decided I had to back off from community involvement when my people weren't there. I had to spend time with the people and die in the wilderness without seeing the promised land if necessary. Now the community organization meets often in the church, and we have been getting involved. The congregation is doing it; I'm not having to lead them directly. They are organizing some block clubs, and another group is working on a community cleanup day. A group from the church went to a meeting the other night on child abuse. We had a series of dinners and invited the alderman, the beat cops, the garbage collectors, the school principals, and the public aid lawyers that we deal with to say thank you for helping serve with us as ministers in this neighborhood. By doing that, we earn the right to critique them. We've begun taking on a local bank, too. We have opened many accounts from the church, and members have recruited some funds from institutions outside Chicago in an attempt to reverse the bank's proven disinvestment in our area, and, eventually, to get some conventional loans for housing in the neighborhood.

If we are to see the urban church revitalized, we have to understand the history of the people who make up that church, and we have to see how they relate to each other within their families. We have to become a part of that church ourselves, building up our credibility. Then together, we can grow and make our shared life felt in the community.

Sixteen

MINISTRY AMONG THE URBAN INDIAN

Dr. Leonard P. Rascher

IT IS VERY IMPORTANT to me to state at the outset that it is *not* my intention to attempt to speak *for* the Native Americans. They are certainly quite capable of speaking for themselves, and they obviously do not need me to try to put words in their mouths. There are on the scene today a number of articulate Native American spokesmen, and we non-Indians who are ministering among Indians need to give careful attention to what they are telling us.

It is my intention to speak *about* some of the issues and concerns of Native Americans, especially as these relate to ministry among them.

Let me also add that I do not consider myself an expert

Leonard P. Rascher

Dr. Rascher is the director of the Practical Christian Work Department and a faculty member of Moody Bible Institute. He formerly served as Dean of Education for Echo Bible Institute, a Bible training school for native Americans.

or an authority on the American Indians; rather, I am in a process of learning about Native Americans. This process began when I was about seven years of age and has continued on until the present.

MISUNDERSTANDINGS AND MISCONCEPTIONS

In talking to non-Indians about Indians over a period of years, several stereotyped opinions and misconceptions have been displayed regarding Native Americans. Let us consider three of the most common of these misunderstandings.

1. *The "Vanishing American" Concept.* Many non-Indians of our day have little or no knowledge about the number of Native Americans presently living in the United States. Some non-Indians believe that there are just a few thousand Native Americans left—a sort of holdover from a past period of history. The fact of the matter is that American Indians today are the fastest growing ethnic population, per capita, of any people in this country. Census figures vary from report to report, but it is conservatively estimated that there are at present some one million to one and one-quarter million full bloods or near full bloods. When counting those of mixed blood who identify themselves as Native American, there may be as many as seven or eight million. The official government census report of 1920 listed 244,437 Native Americans.

When considering Native American population figures, it is important to note the significant trend in American Indian migration to the major urban centers of the country. In 1970 at least one-third of the Indian population was residing in the cities. A 1972 statement issued by the U. S. Government Printing Office declared that:

> Indians have moved in large numbers to metropolitan areas such as New York, Chicago, San Francisco, and Los Angeles. The 1970 census indicated that there are approximately 310,000 Indians in such metropolitan centers. Another 50,000 are in smaller urbanized areas of 2,500 and up.[1]

A 1975 statement by Levitan and Johnston reports that:

> Between 1960 and 1970, the census count of urban Indians more than doubled. . . . On the other hand, the number living in rural areas grew by only 11 percent . . . despite a birth rate that added 52 percent to the total Indian population. . . . By 1970, several cities had larger Indian populations than any reservation except the Navajo.[2]

In 1971 James E. Officer commented, "Indians seem to be moving into the larger cities at a rate considerably in excess of that at which the reservation population is increasing."[3]

By 1976 a little more than 50 percent of all Native Americans were living in cities; one report listed the urban Indian population at 52.6 percent. Although for many, reservation ties remain quite strong and there is considerable mobility back and forth, there are now more Indians living in the cities than there are living on the reservations.

2. The "All Indians Are Alike" Concept. It is true that all Native Americans do share certain commonalities,

but there are also a number of significant tribal differences and distinctions. Politicians, educators, economists, missionaries, and health officials sometimes refer to an "Indian problem" as if there were really only one. Unfortunately, policies are sometimes established, monies appropriated, and programs instituted in an attempt to solve, or at least deal with, such a "problem."

We need to recognize the fact that Native Americans belong to separate and often independent nations of people with very specific and oftentimes unrelated concerns. Tribes have cultural, religious, political, and economic distinctives. Certain of the specific issues faced by the various tribes cannot and should not be lumped together to be dealt with as though they were all the same.

3. *The "Indians Are Just Like Other American Minorities" Concept.* Native Americans are unique from other minorities in America for several reasons. Perhaps the most outstanding difference is the special status they hold with respect to the federal government, a relationship that has been often referred to as "wardship," or "guardianship." In defining the legal status of Indians, the Bureau of Indian Affairs (BIA) states:

> The Federal Government is a trustee of Indian property, not the guardian of the individual Indian. The Secretary of the Interior is authorized by law in many instances to protect the interests of minors and incompetents, but this protection does not confer a guardian-ward relationship.[5]

Although the BIA does not define its relationship to Native Americans as being technically that of wardship; nevertheless, this is exactly how many Indians view it.

Others also view this relationship as one of wardship. In 1968, Robert Kennedy stated:

> Really it's almost like a condition of being owned by the white man and by the Federal Government, the Federal Government being able to decide and determine your own destiny and having a tremendous club over the head of the people, whether it be education, jobs, or whatever.[6]

Another of the more prominent differences that sets Native Americans apart from other minority groups is that of possessing a land base. Some tribes have extensive land holdings. It is virtually impossible to relate to Indians without the discussion having some direct or indirect bearing on their association with and ties to their tribal lands. Very few non-Indians have come to appreciate and understand the Indian's relationship to his land. No other American minority group associates itself to land as does the American Indian.

CONTEMPORARY ISSUES

Three of the basic and prominent issues of concern to the contemporary Native American are identity, self-determination, and urbanization.

• *Identity.* Who is an Indian? Who are the *real* Indians? What does being Indian mean to an Indian? These are difficult and perplexing questions not only for non-Indians to answer but for many Native Americans as well. The BIA gives the following answer:

> There is no general legislative or judicial definition

of "an Indian" that can be used to identify a person as an Indian. A person identified in the United States Census as an Indian generally declares himself to be one. The concept of race as used by the Bureau of the Census does not denote any scientific definition of what race a person identifies with. . . .

To be designated as an Indian eligible for basic Bureau of Indian Affairs services, an individual must live on or near a reservation or on or near trust or restricted land under the jurisdiction of the Bureau, be a member of a tribe, band, or group of Indians recognized by the Federal Government, and for some purposes, be of one-fourth or more Indian descent.[7]

It has been widely stated in much of the current literature treating Native Americans that many Indian youths of today have serious problems with identity. In 1968, August Little Soldier reported to the Senate Hearings that:

The Indian youth of today has a serious identification problem of his own. Extensive psychological testing for four hundred and fifteen young Indian people revealed severe disturbances mostly attributable to a lack of proper identification. . . .

It was seen that the Indian youth is alienated from himself and others. He is not effectively identified with his Indian heritage, nor can he identify with the hostile, white world facing him.[8]

How do most Native Americans identify themselves? Without trying to be too simplistic nor generalizing, I would like to point out four major groups of Native Americans today. For purposes of illustration, we will refer to what may be considered to be the extreme examples in the first two major classifications. We need to recognize, of course, that different people are at different levels in terms of identifying with any one or more of these major groupings.

Tribal or *Traditional.* Sometimes these people have been referred to as the "Long-hairs." These are those Natives who wish to identify with the old ways. Some of these are very idealistic and wish it were somehow possible to relive the good old days before the coming of the white man. Among this group there is a significant return to the old tribal religions.

Assimilated. Sometimes these people have been referred to as "Apples" or "Uncle Tom-Toms" or "Uncle Tomahawks." These are those Natives who have largely given up their Indian identity and have opted to live like the white man. They recognize their tribal descent but have exchanged Indian values and customs for those of the dominant society, and they have adopted the white middle-class life-style as their own.

Marginals. Sometimes these people have been referred to as "misfits." These are those Natives who recognize themselves to be suspended somewhere in between the Indian and the white cultures. They move back and forth between the two, but generally are not fully accepted into either.

Neo-Natives. Sometimes these people have been referred to as "pan-Indians." These are those Natives that Steiner referred to as the "New Indians." They have a more definite sense of Indian identity than do the Marginals, and they are also more realistic than some of the Traditionals in that they know it is impossible to relive all of the old tribal ways. Nor do they want to be assimilated into the dominant white society. They want to remain Indian and at the same time enjoy the best of both worlds.

• *Self-Determination.* One can hardly talk to Indian leaders today or read about current Indian affairs without coming across the term *self-determination.* Native American leaders today are vocal, and rightfully so, in declaring their right to decide their own destiny.

In 1969 the United Southeastern Tribes issued a policy statement in which they declared that the role of the Indian and the role of the federal government toward each other should

> *not* be defined as a partnership, but rather that *the Indian be recognized as the controller of his own destiny both in terms of the direction he chooses and the method of moving in that direction.* . . .
>
> In summary, what we ask for Indian people is "self-development," with emphasis equally distributed between "self" and "development." We do not want development to be something which is done *to* us but something done *by* us. We want our own goals, attitudes, and cherished beliefs to be expressed in the way in which we develop.[9]

In pursuing self-determination, the issue is not whether Indian leaders will call for change or not; the issue is, will they or will they not have control over the decisions that affect whatever change is to occur?

Levitan and Johnston concluded their text on Native Americans by stating: "Ultimately, Indians must decide the future course of their culture. Federal policy . . . must at last leave the resolution of 'the Indian question' to Indians."[10]

● *Urbanization.* Why are such large numbers of Native Americans migrating to the cities? Individual answers to this question are many and varied. The more common reasons are: to secure jobs, to escape overcrowding and hardship on the reservations, to provide a better education for the children, to relocate among friends and/or relatives who moved to the city.

What do Native Americans find when they move to the city? Often they find that the problems they tried to leave behind are not only still with them, but have grown to crisis proportions. There are numerous internal and external pressures that bear down on Native Americans who are transplanted into the city. Most of these pressures are ones over which they have little or no control, and these usually make adjusting to the urban way of life very difficult if not almost impossible. Many of these same pressures still apply to second- and third-generation urban Natives.

The following diagram illustrates how some of these pressures exert influence upon the urban Indian.

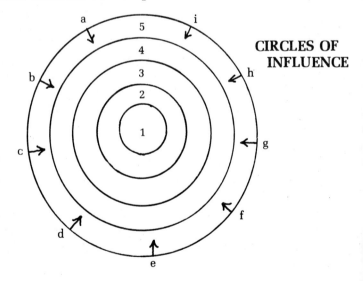

CIRCLES OF INFLUENCE

1. The center circle represents an individual urban Indian. Circles two through five represent those areas that
exert influence upon the individual.
2. The second circle represents the Indian family,
which exerts the greatest degree of influence upon the
individual. This group includes not only his immediate
family but grandparents, aunts and uncles, and cousins.
Even if the Indian is in the city without his family, he
still feels their influence to some degree. Among some
tribes there is something of a family breakdown occurring, but generally the family is still quite influential.
3. The third circle represents the Indian community.
On the reservation, this would primarily be one's own
tribe. In the city, the community could include not only
members of one's own tribe but also members of several
tribes. Often Indians outside one's family or tribe can
and do exercise considerable influence upon the urban
Indian.
4. The fourth circle represents the Bureau of Indian
Affairs, even though the extent of the BIA's influence is
far greater on the reservation Indian than on the urban
Indian. That influence sometimes extends to second-
and third-generation urban Natives, as in the case of
providing federal assistance for higher education.
5. The outer circle represents the non-Indian community at large. Some of the primary influences include:
    a. *Economics.* If it is true that many Native Ameri-
cans migrate to the city to find jobs, what happens when
they get to the city? It should be noted that there are
practically no Native-run businesses in the city. Indians
must compete in an open job market with many others
looking for the same job. Many Indians are either unskilled or semiskilled and find themselves improperly
trained for some of the available jobs. Native Americans
often find themselves targets of both individual and

institutionalized discrimination when they apply for jobs. A disproportionate number of American Indians end up working for day-labor outfits.

b. *Education.* Do urban Indian children receive a better education than their reservation counterparts? Not according to some of the available research, in which many Native American parents expressed the opinion that their children could get a better education "back home."

c. *Housing.* What housing is available to the urban Indian? For the most part, slum housing. Many Indians have to find nonlease housing when they move to the city, and usually what they find is in a ghetto.

d. *Health and Welfare.* Generally speaking, urban Indians are not eligible for federal health care while they live in the city. Usually they are required to attend whatever city health care clinics are available, and many times they are discriminated against in these clinics. Some Natives are forced to return to their reservations for federal health care attention. Unlike the reservation situation, welfare assistance is distributed in the city in centers not exclusively set up for Indians, and here again Native Americans have become targets of discrimination.

e. *Politics.* Most urban Indians do not register and vote. In Chicago, there are presently no Indian aldermen or precinct captains. Urban Indian concerns are, therefore, not generally represented in the city's government.

f. *Law.* Because of alcoholism, evictions, etc., many urban Indians find themselves in trouble with the law. Most of the relationships that Indians have with law enforcement officials tend to be negative ones.

g. *Media.* The media usually treat Native Americans in either a patronizing way or they tend to stereotype them in cartoons and/or biased articles.

h. *Religion.* Many Indians do not feel welcome in most of the urban churches. A number of Natives have expressed to me, over the years, that they are made to feel uncomfortable, conspicuous, and unwanted when they have attended European-American churches.

i. *Culture.* Many of the values and customs of the urban dominant community are foreign to and considerably different from those of the Indian. For example, many Natives value giving and sharing and find it hard to live in a dog-eat-dog, highly competitive urban society.

BASIC PRINCIPLES FOR EFFECTIVE CROSS-CULTURAL COMMUNICATION

What means do we have for effectively ministering among urban Indians? I can suggest nine basic principles that have application in most cross-cultural situations.

1. *Be informed.* We need to learn all we can about the urban Indian community and the different tribes that make up the community. What is happening today in the community? Who is doing the speaking for the Indians? Who does he/she represent? What is he/she saying? We need to continually be students of the people: find out what they want, then guide them in it; don't come at them just with what you want.

2. *Be yourself.* We need to be real and not try to put on qualities that are not genuine. Especially we need to be absolutely honest, never being guilty of speaking with a "forked tongue."

3. *Be flexible.* We need to be ready to adapt, modify and/or change. Remember, our way may not necessarily

be either the *right* way or the *only* way.

4. *Be sensitive.* We need to train ourselves to observe others' feelings and ideas. We have to be careful not to violate cultural customs and differences.

5. *Emphasize the universality of Christ's atonement.* Christ is not just the white man's God. We need to make it clear that Christianity is not just another religion in competition with all of the others. Emphasize that Christianity is having a personal relationship with the very God of the universe.

6. *Learn their language.* This takes hard work and much discipline. If you are working with more than one tribe, learn as much of each different language as you can. Use different tribal words in explaining and teaching the Word of God.

7. *Learn their value systems.* We need to identify and distinguish primary, secondary, and tertiary values.

8. *Contextualize the message.* We can best communicate the Word of God by relating it to concepts familiar to Native cultures. Look for what Don Richardson calls, "redemptive analogies."

9. *Communicate according to their thought patterns.* Learn to communicate with illustrations, diagrams, and storytelling. Teach by demonstration, not by explanation. Use appropriate gestures and other nonverbal techniques and express yourself in ideas that are compatible with their thought patterns.

REFERENCES

1. Taylor, Theodore W., *The States and Their Indian Citizens* (Washington: U. S. Government Printing Office, 1972), pp. 77-78.
2. Levitan, S. and Johnston, W., *Indian Giving: Federal Programs for Native Americans* (Baltimore: John Hopkins University Press, 1975), pp. 2-3.

3. Waddell, J. and Watson, O., *The American Indian in Urban Society* (Boston: Little, Brown & Co., 1971), pp. 55-56.

4. Levitan and Johnston, *Indian Giving*, p. 4.

5. Answers To Questions: *The American Indian: Answers to 101 Questions* (Washington: U. S. Department of Interior Bureau of Indian Affairs, U. S. Government Printing Office, 1974), p. 6.

6. Senate Hearings: *Indian Education*. (Washington: U. S. Government Printing Office, 1969), p. 1234.

7. Answers to Questions, *The American Indian*, p. 2.

8. Senate Hearings: *Indian Education*, p. 1256.

9. "A Policy Statement of the United Southeastern Tribes Regarding Federal Legislation Affecting the Indian People." Albuquerque: ABC: *Americans Before Columbus*, National Indian Youth Council. 1969, p. 11.

10. Levitan and Johnston, *Indian Giving*, p. 80.

Seventeen

URBAN CHURCH EVANGELISM IN A MULTIETHNIC SOCIETY

James Conklin

THE URBAN CHURCH finds itself in the midst of poverty, broken families, ethnic polarities, unemployment, poor schools, fear, violence, and crime. These problems have broken and destroyed many once-great ministries. Yet all around are people. Our challenge is to discover where God is at work and then link up with him to revitalize the church's evangelistic efforts.

We live with a stereotype that says Christianity is monoethnic. Oh, the church may rent its facilities out to other racial groups for worship or special meetings, but seldom does it invite those people to become part and parcel of the congregation, to share ownership of God's building. Typically, this same church sees itself as im-

James E. Conklin
  Dr. Conklin is general coordinator and pastor of the English congregation of Temple Baptist Church, Los Angeles. Temple Church is a multiethnic unit made up of four different congregations: English, Hispanic, Korean, and Chinese.

minently relevant to the city of which it is a part, while the people in the city would say it is completely irrelevant.

The society of the city-center, however, is pluralistic. Equal-housing and equal-opportunity laws, together with integrated education and other institutions will homogenize our society further each year.

If the church is to remain vital in a pluralistic society, it must (1) reflect the community of which it is a part; (2) open its doors to equal participation and membership by all; (3) affirm and integrate each person and ethnic group into the one Body of Christ; (4) develop a trust and love between family members and, more broadly, ethnic bodies, thus strengthening the moral fabric of the community and nation; and (5) reduce the exorbitant cost of multiplying monoethnic buildings that take valuable funds needed for meeting human need.

Temple Church in Los Angeles was a church that had grown and had been effective in the inner city. But then the people surrounding the church moved to the suburbs, and people from a variety of races and cultures moved in. Our church began to die in its immigrant society. Language and cultural barriers hemmed us in.

What we all need to realize, of course, is that every one of us is an immigrant—even the Indians came from other countries. That puts us on an equal basis; no one can call someone else a foreigner. We are all either in the process of acculturation, that is, borrowing from the society of which we are a part, taking on new models and forms; or of "inculturation," holding on to old forms, language, ways of thought, and mores. The tension between those two has always fractured the Christian church.

Because the church was dying, the congregation had a self-image of defeat and death and despair and weakness. That was a necessary step in the growth process, because change cannot take place if we feel the direction we are going is right. Change can only take place in a condition of stress.

Then we asked, "Why is the church here? If we're here to win people to Christ, is our job done?" Someone has pointed out that the action verb in the Great Commission is not "go" or "baptize" or "teach"—those are participles. The action verb is "make disciples." Disciples are people who are trained, then involved in doing the task.

The question then, was what does it mean for a monoethnic church dying in the heart of a great city to make disciples? It means change; it means that either we change or we die. Anyone going to an inner-city church should have in mind what he wants to do before he gets there. It would be highly advantageous for him to live in the church a year or two and analyze the church and how the congregation feels about itself, before he accepts a call to be pastor.

Once a church recognizes its weaknesses, it can begin to develop a positive self-image. Members of a church need to know who they are and who they can become. Then they need to have something that binds them together. In our case, we developed a prayer covenant and designed a little pin to remind us of our commitment and identity.

Our church had at that point about four-hundred, English-speaking people coming to worship, a growing Spanish department, a small Korean congregation that was using our facilities because their building had burned down, and a Chinese congregation. I asked the official board of the English-speaking congregation to allow us to act in a multicongregational way by treating the other congregations as equals and setting up an ad hoc multicongregational committee to develop a charter statement. This move was crucial, because the church of the inner city must be multiethnic. If it's going to be a community, the church must be made up of the people who live there (and our denominational tags will become increasingly irrelevant).

The point of having a multiethnic church is that all groups are first class; no one congregation predominates; and no language or cultural group loses its authenticity. We need at least two congregations within the English-speaking group, because we have two subcultural groups—a younger and an older. There are certain forms of worship that speak to young people that do not communicate to the older generation and vice versa. So let them have their own congregation within the church. When the need for it has passed, it will die.

The charter statement, which took us two years to write, tries to recognize the differences between groups. It is the glue that holds us all together. Our purposes in this multicongregational church are to build community, solve the problem of the fractured family, and then erode the roots of crime and violence. When we find ourselves, we can project out to another person and say "I love you." When our love gets on a deeper level of commitment than eating together or watching the same TV show or sharing the same house, then we are going to start considering the consequences of our actions on other people. The family that shares and talks about its faith is not as likely to have one of its members going out and committing a crime. We all should have learned a lesson from *Roots*: Chicken George didn't know who he was, so how could he know where he was going? Isn't that true of all of us? If we don't have a sense of identity, how do we know what purposes God has for us?

The organizational structure of our church does not

provide for a monolithic giant that is dictating to all the other groups what they should do. What we have instead is a mechanism for dealing with mutual concerns on an equal basis. Committees report to a general coordinating council. Part of that council is an ex officio, pastoral advisory board made up of all the pastors serving the various congregations. At the center is an activator, a general coordinator—not a bishop or some other authority figure.

We need to live in a large community as a church so that we will know how to live in a city and relate to the people there. We lack knowledge about how to relate to people from different cultures. We mistakenly think that living in this melting-pot country of ours makes us all alike, but it doesn't. We need to learn to treat people in terms of their own self-identity instead of in terms of what we think they should be and do. As we learn to relate to each other, we will open the floodgates of evangelism and allow people to respond to Jesus Christ authentically.

When we think about evangelistic methods for the urban church, we must take into account the influence of the particular cultural unit on an individual's religious decision. The Koreans with whom I worked in northern Thailand, for example, might raise their hand in a meeting to please the missionary. But those decisions were not genuine, because religion for them, as all important aspects of life, is based on decisions made by the whole village as a group. So you somehow have to bring the village to a point of stress, of recognizing weaknesses in their system, and then show them the hope that is in Jesus Christ. Once the village has been won, individuals may be won. It takes some time to recognize the cultural unit to whom you are ministering, but that understanding is essential.

Another crucial step in effective evangelism is to bring people to a stress condition. The people with whom we share need to see us and what we have as at least a partial solution to their needs or problems before they will give a listening ear.

So, for instance, we could ask the members of our congregation to write down the names of five friends who are not church-goers. Then, where do you know them? On the job? School? Leisure time? Playing golf or some other sport? We are seeking to find out the point at which we have a shared experience.

Then we ask, what do we know of their value system? Are they more concerned about dents in their car than they are in the health of their kids? Many people are. When that value system is threatened, a stress condition exists. For instance, when a guy who really loves his car is in a bad accident, you know he's in a stress condition. You may care nothing about a dent, but you have to realize that that guy is not the same as he was yesterday. He is suffering, really hurting. He needs to be touched at the moment of his perceived stress condition. If you do come in at the point of his value system, then you can begin to touch him effectively for Christ. You might, in this case, loan him your car. That could make a tremendous difference in his attitude toward you. Then you could share something new in the way of a value system.

So the church needs to set up an evangelism program that fits the needs of its community and is culturally true. Then we will have a hearing.

PART FOUR
Resources

Eighteen

STRATEGIES FOR URBAN RECONSTRUCTION

Stanley Hallett

ONE OF THE PROBLEMS of thinking about the city is that every time you get up in the morning you feel as if the kaleidoscope has turned and all the parts have fallen into another shape and you have to start all over again. Part of what we have been trying to do at Northwestern's Center for Urban Affairs is to identify some guideposts that can be used to think about where the urban city is headed so we can develop strategies to shape a different kind of city than we now live in.

Change is certain. But the directions and nature of that change, whether it will be the unintended outcome of human action or the result of purposeful planning, is the central question. It might be more fun to start talking

Stanley James Hallett

Dr. Hallett is a lecturer in policy and environment for the Graduate School of Management and the Urban Affairs Center of Northwestern University. He is a vice-president of South Shore National Bank.

about the specifics—how to grow tomatoes in a rooftop greenhouse on the West Side—but I would rather start from generalities and identify the major changes that are occurring.

Let's begin by looking at the tool kit, or the technology, that is currently being used to supply the urban city so we can think of how that kit might be restructured. At one time, towns functioned in a natural cycle, much like the environment of a village in Bavaria. From four hundred to six hundred years old, these villages nestle in little valleys where they use the sunlight, rain, wind, and soil to sustain human life. What the village takes out of its environment, it puts back in. The waste from households goes back onto the land; the energy from trees and the soil goes into building houses. There is a natural set of parameters through which these villages interact with nature.

But a funny thing happened on the way to the modern, industrial city. The development of specialized production required that factories be built at the points where goods could be transported. For the nineteenth-century village, that meant where the railhead hit the harbor. But with new means of transportation, new sources of energy, and new possibilities for concentrated production and specialization, cities in the twentieth century began to spread out and develop increasingly specialized functions. The International Harvester plant in Peoria, Illinois, for example, manufactures farm implements, only one part of a system that finally comes together on an Illinois or Iowa farm and is later processed, preserved, packaged, transported, and finally distributed to the point where it reaches our breakfast table. This system is increasingly chain-linked, remotely controlled, and vulnerable, with only one output. And the same thing goes for waste. Once you turn the little handle, the waste starts down into a long, complex set of tubes, pipes, tunnels, and treatment plants, and is finally dumped out into the water or onto the land.

In fact, we are in the process of destroying our own water supply. When we build large shopping centers with huge parking lots, we increase the runoff of rain water by 100 percent. This decreases the water's infiltration into the soil, which means we stop recharging the underground resources that we are at the same time tapping for well water.

Now we are proposing to build a mega-set of tools to solve the problems we have created. In order to manage the wastes of the city (Chicago alone generates about 4 million pounds of human waste a day and about three times that much in other solid wastes), we are starting to build huge tunnels thirty feet in diameter about two hundred feet underground at a cost of 6-to-7 billion dollars. Having generated tools that act like a tornado, sucking the resources out of one place and spewing them onto another, we are now in the process of deciding how to build an even bigger set of tools to make this process work faster so we can deal with rising costs.

But another way to approach this would be to ask, Is there any way to reconstruct a tool set so it works naturally within the life of a community? For instance, maybe we could develop a mini-set of tools, like an anaerobic digester out behind a unit of housing that would convert human waste and garbage into methane to be used for cooking or into nutrients that could be used in a greenhouse.

We should always be trying to get the cycle working again so we are putting resources to work rather than depleting them. And when we think of doing that, we need to try and create the necessary jobs in the neighborhoods where people need work.

Part of what makes a neighborhood function successfully is personal income so people can pay their taxes and maintain the operating costs of quasipublic activities such as hospitals, schools, public offices, and libraries. As families earn money, they put it into financial institutions, and these banks provide the credit that is needed for the community to stay alive and renew itself. The extension of credit is an extension of trust that enables people to get a stake in their community and get equity in their housing.

But a strange thing sometimes happens to neighborhoods. Because the housing supply is fixed, if the population or the demand for housing drops a bit, the inelastic supply of houses and the elastic demand will exaggerate a decline in price that makes financial institutions nervous. So they shut off the flow of credit.

This loss has a significant effect on the life of the community. In the South Shore area of Chicago, a neighborhood that was totally redlined by financial institutions in 1972, about three hundred jobs have been lost in housing maintenance alone. Owners felt that "if we can't sell our property because nobody can get credit to buy it and we can't get our money out, why should we maintain it?"

Soon the government had to put increased expenditures into family income maintenance, unemployment, welfare compensation, and social security. And the maintenance costs, such as police services, start to achieve less and less, because once a community becomes unstable it is almost impossible to police.

As the economy in a neighborhood begins to shift, the second, third, or fourth jobs in a family are affected. This doesn't mean much if the father is making $20,000 or $30,000. But if he's making $6,000, another $2,000 or

RESOURCES

$3,000 makes an enormous difference.

Since 1970, an hourglass pattern has developed. Families that make it through the neck of the hourglass, which is an income of about $8,000, go on up in income level. But families below that have been pushed back into poverty. There's been a decrease in the income of people on welfare by 16 percent since 1974, and that's from a very small initial base.

At the same time, you have an upward spiral in the suburbs. Developers are building new houses and commercial structures, and the government is pumping capital-improvements money into highways, water, sewer, public facilities, and schools to create a new community. That, in turn, is generating jobs, local income, and demands for housing.

In stable communities, deposits flow into financial institutions, and loans come back. Taxes are paid, and money is available to support public sector activities. In a redlined community, however, the money flows out, and the lines to get it back are gone. The local financial institution ships the money off to the regional money centers, like downtown banks. The area continues to deteriorate, and the local financial institutions shrink and leave the community. There are three hundred thousand black people on the west side of Chicago, and there is not one financial institution between Halsted and Austin.

If one looks at the Chicago region as a whole, money is flowing out of these communities and into the suburbs. Because of the disclosure laws that were passed about three years ago, money flow can actually be tracked. We know, for instance, that Continental and First National Bank have a total of $31 million on deposit from residents of the South Shore and only $76,000 back in loans. Now that's a very efficient vacuum cleaner, sucking the money out of the community and pumping it into investments in the suburbs and the Bahamas.

Recently, we estimated what it would cost to turn South Shore around and make it once again a first-rate neighborhood. Our estimates included a large, new shopping center, three smaller, convenient shopping centers, rehabilitation of 20 percent of the houses, redoing the old South Shore Country Club, and building two new schools. The total cost came to $120 million, the same amount that South Shore people had on deposit in banks. All they needed to turn their neighborhood around was to recycle their own money. But to destroy it, to let it go the route of a number of other Chicago neighborhoods, would mean the government would be pumping in an excess of $500 million. And they'd have to put in another half billion in order to rebuild that same neighborhood in a cornfield. A total of a billion dollars' worth of government money, plus twice that much private capital and credit, in order to destroy the central city and build it in the suburbs.

The fact is we are doing just that at the rate of one neighborhood a year. We're building twenty-five thousand dwelling units a year in the suburbs and destroying twenty-five thousand units in the city. The macroeconomists who try to deal with the problems of inflation and depression at the same time are ignoring the fact that they are parts of a simultaneous boom/bust cycle in our urban regions. Most of the proposed activities of the macroeconomists will only stimulate this activity and increase the pace at which it occurs.

The costs to the churches involved in urban neighborhoods are enormous. In any neighborhood of eighty-thousand people, there are about 10 million dollars of church buildings; most of which will be abandoned and destroyed this wholesale transformation.

RESOURCES

So far, I've posed a lot of questions. Now I'd like to suggest a few ways churches might begin to deal with these problems. The church's primary function should be to create forums to discuss these changes and ways of dealing with them.

The church can participate in models to show what can be done. For instance, a number of churches invested in a South Shore bank, and that bank now has 15 million dollars' worth of loans in the South Shore neighborhood, with a lower default rate than the average at the First National Bank.

The church can also encourage a discussion of how some of the mega-tool investments can be stopped. If Commonwealth Edison builds $4.3 billion worth of nuclear power plants by 1982, we're going to have to pay for that, whether we use them or not. If the metropolitan sanitary district builds those deep tunnels, we'll pay for that, too. But we have the option of developing tools that are locally owned. One thing about solar energy rather than nuclear energy is that once it's in place, it's paid for.

In Norway families are given a piece of shore for fishing, a piece of land to farm, wood to get their heat from, and a place for a house. Let's say each person in our cities had five hundred square feet of indoor space that was free of taxes and had enough sunlight to grow food and get heat. With that base, the worst thing that could happen if a person got fired, would be that he'd stay home and tend his greenhouse. We need to see if there's some kind of base like that to depressurize our whole system.

Instead of pressing for increased maintenance grants and public service jobs, which I think are dead ends, we should begin to focus on the tools and techniques that are now being used and look for ones that might take their place. The federal government spends $30 billion a year on research and development, two-thirds of the research and development money in the nation. Community and church groups have not put any pressure on that budget.

The Center for Neighborhood Technology in Chicago has been putting together a coalition of community groups to make demands on some of that funding and channel it into urban neighborhoods so local groups can get the technical resources and know-how as well as the capital and credit to rebuild their neighborhoods.

I would also suggest that churches look through their portfolios, their endowments and pension funds. If they find bank stock, they could make that portfolio policy sensitive rather than neutral. If the bank is currently involved in redlining or investing outside of the community, suggest that it reconsider these policies. A set of proposals is now before the Proxmire committee that would create incentive for banks to move more aggressively on neighborhood reinvestment.

A church can organize with other groups in the neighborhood to demand that banks begin to take responsibility in the community. People should keep going into the bank and saying, "If this area isn't credit worthy, tell us what would change that," and demand that they come up with some data. One of the things we are finding is that the credit judgment of these institutions is not based on a calculated, mathematical model that is drawn from an empirical data base but racial, ethnic, and class-colored glasses.

Finally, let me make clear the type of technical change I'm suggesting. We've been through a period of heavy technology, and the nature of that technology has been socially determined. When Monsanto was trying to decide where to go because the oil companies were diving into petrochemicals, they said, "Let's take a look at agriculture." They investigated two alternatives—bugs that would control pests or insecticides, pesticides, and chemicalized fertilizers. The problem with the bugs was that if you turned them loose in one field, they automatically went on to the next and the next. You couldn't sell them, because they went there naturally and dealt with the problem. Whereas if you sprayed, you had to spray each field and then come back next year and spray again. You had a built-in market.

I'm not suggesting that we reject technology, but that we pass from a period of heavy technology into a period of light technology, which might be just as sophisticated if not more so. We've been through a period of engineers and chemists, and I'm suggesting that we go into a period of biologists, that we move from a chain-linked, remotely controlled, vulnerable system toward a more natural cycle like that of the Bavarian village.

Nineteen

CONSULTATION FOR ASSISTANCE IN DEVELOPING URBAN MINISTRY

Philip Amerson

URBAN CHURCHES ARE OFTEN drowning amid a sea of resources. How can churches better investigate, analyze, strategize, implement, and evaluate for mission? Consultation services, where urban congregations work together and assist one another in a planning process, are one answer.

By consultation I mean an exchange or a sharing of resources among urban churches and those who have special expertise so that a congregation can better know and employ its mission. Most typically, urban churches need consultation not because they are resourceless, but because they need to discover and perhaps redirect the many resources they already have.

Philip A. Amerson
Dr. Amerson is a member of the Patchwork Central Ministering Community in Evansville, working particularly as consultant in education and research.

RESOURCES

Informal styles of consultation have always been a vital part of urban ministry as pastors or laypersons exchange a "Let me tell you how we solved that problem," or "Have you ever run across this issue or organization before?" What we are lacking is a clearinghouse where specific resources can be directed to specific needs within a congregation, and a method that would supply good research to urban parishes at a reasonable cost.

Specifically, consultation services are needed to shed light on four shadows that threaten many of our city churches—perspective, resources, focus, and appropriate goals and strategies. Lack of perspective is most often a matter of scale: "The problems are too large, and we are so small." This often involves a theological crisis as well, one that requires people to answer the question, "Why are we here, and what is the place of our church in this city?" Redlining and disinvestment have undoubtedly been practiced by most of the major institutions of our society—banks, insurance companies, school corporations, and yes, even church denominations. Yet, one is often struck by the failure of urban congregations to recognize and employ the many resources they have. Thus, clouded perspective and a distorted inventory of their resources result in a blurred focus of the congregation's mission.

Finally, consultation would often be valuable in assisting congregations to establish realistic goals and strategies. One of the most pressing needs of the urban parish is to establish short-range goals, where people accomplish tasks, recognize themselves as "winners," and take time to celebrate their victories.

There are four main reasons why churches have had little experience with consultation. First, research and the time to be reflective about urban church needs have been low priorities for both our local churches and our denominations. Just as realtors live out certain myths that often become self-fulfilling in blighted areas, so church leaders expect a demise or lack of vitality in urban churches.

One can understand that the day-to-day frustrations and demands on an urban parish might cause research and goal setting to be given low priority. But because of the investment we have already made and the potential we have to discover, one wonders why denominational bodies fail to assist their urban congregations in looking at questions beyond survival.

Secondly, there is a fear of the expense. But research costs can be reduced by churches combining to collect basic data, much of which is already available.

A third factor is the experience of bad or inappropriate research. We joke about college students who are ready to act as qualified psychiatrists after an Introduction to Psychology course, and the same problem exists in social research. Most congregations have not done the sufficient groundwork and are not blessed with persons who have adequate research skills.

Finally, there is little awareness of the many good consultation services that are available to the church.

I would like to suggest an elementary planning process that could be used by congregations to do community research. It is composed of five stages: involvement, analysis, strategy, implementation, and evaluation. The process begins with an involvement in the community. Before a church can know where analysis is needed, it must know the community.

Next a church should become aware of the valuable information that is already available. I would suggest that congregations take one-to-two years gathering the available research before attempting an inventory of their own. Before one knows what questions should be asked, one needs to know the information already available. The list below includes the places to begin gathering information.

1. Census data—by census tract and blocks
2. Census data updates—from the city directory (Published by R. L. Polk, 6400 Monroe Blvd., Box 500, Taylor, MI 48180)
3. Most neighborhood libraries must do extensive research on the community they serve to receive certain funding. This is an extremely productive source of information.
4. U. S. Department of Labor for statistics
5. City and regional departments of planning
6. Public health departments
7. Departments of community development and redevelopment commissions
8. Public school research
9. Marketing research groups (For television, radio, and consumer products, companies like Minnesota Mining and Manufacturing and Proctor & Gamble do extensive research, often broken by census tracts.)
10. Nearby universities, especially business and sociology schools

There are many other sources, and while it might take work to gain access to some of this information, most of it is given free to the public.

It may be appropriate for the local parish to ask for a basic inventory of the congregation. There are several research groups who can assist in this process. Three inventories are already available that give congregations a comprehensive overview of themselves at a relatively low cost.

SUGGESTED INVENTORIES

Parish Profile Inventory
Church and Ministry Program
Hartford Seminary Foundation
55 Elizabeth St.
Hartford, CT 06105

Parish Evaluation Project
National Federation of Priests Councils Office
1307 South Wabash Ave.
Chicago, IL 60605

Church Membership Inventory
Office of Research
United Church Board of Homeland Ministries
287 Park Ave. South
New York, NY 10010

One way to begin developing consultation skills would be for twenty or thirty churches in a neighborhood or denominational area to band together and agree to identify those clergy and laypersons who would be qualified to serve as consultants for the whole group on specific issues. Another is to provide the money to train some people in the areas that are needed. This is already being done in many denominations on issues as varied as pension programs and clergy education. But we have not done this sufficiently on issues of urban ministry.

A second part of developing consultation would be for an organization (a denomination or seminary) to serve as a clearinghouse for churches needing consultation assistance. Consultation services could then be offered to churches by a group such as SCUPE.

RESOURCES

MODEL FOR CHURCH CONSULTATION

1. *Preliminary discussions.* These would be necessary between the consulting team and the church or churches to determine what the primary interests are—goal setting, organizational development, conflict management, resourcing projects, or evangelism. Costs for this would be minimal (postage, telephone calls), except when on-the-site preparation was necessary.

2. *Initial data collection and computer analysis.* The instruments I have previously identified are available to assist congregations in doing an introductory inventory on both the congregation and the surrounding community. The cost for such analysis would vary, depending on the number of churches participating and the length of the questionnaire, but it would probably be from $150 to $300 per church.

3. *Style of analysis and strategy.* Once computer runs are available, the consultant would work with a team from the church or churches in at least three sessions. The first session would be an explanation and analysis of the initial data, along with the identification and collection of further information. The second session would establish priorities and identify existing or potential blockages. The final session would assist in setting up a means of implementation.

Research work would be carried out by both parties between consulting sessions. A contract would be negotiated with the existing leadership of the congregation making clear the responsibilities of the consultant as well as the congregation. Church leadership would probably be involved in basic data collection and analysis.

4. *Expenses.* Expense for such a service could vary greatly depending on the size and scope of the project.

Costs would probably range from $450 for a single church employing one consultant to $5000 or more for a long-term project involving many churches.

For churches that are interested in consultation, here is a list of pertinent literature:

Amerson, Philip A., "A Resource Packet for the Urban Congregation," *Occasional Papers of the Patchwork Community.* Patchwork Central, 431 Washington Avenue, Evansville, IN 47713. $4.50 per packet. (The packet will contain such resources as: "A Beginning Inventory of Church and Community for Urban Congregations," "An Inventory of Institutional Racism," "A Checklist for Churches in Racial Transition," "Sample Resources of an Organizing Effort to Save a Core-City School.")

Bryand, Marcus, and Kemp, Charles. *The Church and Community Resources.* Bethany Press, 1977.

Cosby, Gordon. *Handbook for Mission Groups.* Word, 1975.

Mead, Loren. *New Hope for Congregations.* Seabury, 1972.

Noyce, Gaylord. *Survival and Mission for the City Church.* Westminister Press, 1975.

Swanson, Bert E. and Edith, *Discovering the Community.* Halsted Press, 1977.

Warren, Rachell B., and Warren, Donald I., *The Neighborhood Organizer's Handbook.* University of Notre Dame Press, 1977.

Twenty

MINISTRY RESOURCES
IN COMMUNITY SYSTEMS

William Ipema

CHICAGO IS SUPPOSED TO BE a city that works, a city of neighborhoods and balanced budgets. Yet it is estimated that thirty-six of our seventy-six communities are fairly dysfunctional, using the green flow in a community as criterion to determine dysfunction. Capital, or green flow, is necessary for life, like the red blood flow through our bodies. How much credit and capital funding, in terms of home mortgages, rehabilitation mortgages, remodeling, and capital investments is available to our urban neighborhoods? Not much. In some communities, less than 1 percent of savings money goes back into the community in the form of loans. Nor are insurance companies issuing policies to

William Ipema

Mr. Ipema is operation director of Chicago Orleans Housing Corporation, a cooperative effort of five neighborhood churches to provide racially and economically integrated housing for more than three-hundred family units on Chicago's Near North Side.

homeowners in these neighborhoods, which is another indicator they have reached a high level of dysfunction.

Urban ministry has become very costly, because the human need in these dysfunctional neighborhoods is so great and the support systems, such as banks, businesses, and insurance companies have been withdrawn. On top of this, urban ministry tends to be underfunded, because many churches and denominations have left the communities and/or others have put urban ministry low on their list of priorities.

As an urban minister I faced these problems, and the only way I was able to cope with them was to become aware of the social service systems and utilize them to help my parishioners. No one is going to solve urban problems by expanding the social service system as is sometimes suggested. We've got to use the agencies that now exist, and try to change them where necessary.

I'd like to suggest ways this can be done by the minister who acts as a referral agent and by the church that builds programs and neighborhood resources within a community. There are hosts of agencies within an urban area, but urban pastors are often not using these services. They tend to be so caught up in the immediate needs of the day that they don't have time to build coalitions and understand the processes of entry into the agencies.

In last year's social service directory (which is available from the United Way for ten dollars) there are 2,260 agencies in the city of Chicago. But when I was ministering in Chicago, I knew of about ten, and was only familiar with the entree process into seven of them. Finally after eight years of urban ministry, I served on one agency board, the only time I had the opportunity to study an agency's policies and regulations and offer suggestions for change.

RESOURCES

One of the problems with social service systems is attitude—ours and theirs. At first, I thought of the folks in those agencies as the enemy. They sat behind their desks pushing paper and really weren't interested in the needs of the community. And this is the impression social service people expect ministers to have.

But then I began to ask myself, *What ever happened to those energetic, visionary, social work graduates? Do they all become fat bureaucrats in just a couple of years?* No, I decided, but they do become depressed, disillusioned, and desperately in need of friends in the community. Maybe if they had some reinforcement from pastors and church folk, they might continue to be visionaries. Now I know there are lots of problems with the system—like thirteen copies of every case report— that cause disillusionment as well. But if we expected them to help us, and provided a climate where they could, these young people might be our allies.

We need to know the location of these agencies, the services they are supposed to provide, and what the entree procedure is so we know how a member of our parish might apply for help. Then we need to get to know the staff, interact with them, and serve on their boards. I'm not necessarily suggesting that urban pastors themselves do all this, but they and the urban folk in their churches and communities could. We need to get on boards that set policy and evaluate services to keep these systems functioning to improve the quality of life in our areas.

A minister should form a relationship with a contact person in an agency. Find out something about this person before you make an appointment to see him or her. Be concerned about the whole individual, not just his or her job. Get to know that individual outside the professional context. Obviously you will also research the agency itself, trying to find out its referral mechanics and other details of its operation. Finally, if you know enough, list the needs you and your parishioners might be able to help them with.

If you go into an agency and say, "I'm pastor so-and-so, and I came here to see what we can do to help you," the response is usually great. These people are not used to hearing that. Often they will open up and share with you on a give-and-take basis. You'll find that the agency needs volunteers for one thing or another, and eventually the agency will need board people who can give some direction.

While you are in the agency, you can uncover new contacts and ideas. Make an appointment with someone at your own professional level. If a minister always goes below his level, he's not going to get the type of interchange he's looking for. And if he always asks to see the director, he's not going to get many appointments. But if he gets to know a middle-level person, by the time the pastor is maturing in his community, this person might be directing the agency's work. Of course, there's always the chance he may have moved on, which means the pastor has to begin again. But it is likely that this middle-level person is a person with whom the minister can grow.

Be sure you don't alienate these people. They are weary of having to make thirteen copies of everything, and they're not stimulated by someone who comes in and right away tells them how to run things.

I believe the church has a better opportunity to build the quality of life in these neighborhoods than it has had for a long time. The activists who rejected the church are by and large gone. New attitudes are developing about church participation in community involvement. The current political administration is much more open to the church. I see people moving directly from positions representing the church into the political systems without even removing their collars. Monsignor Geno Baroni, for instance, serves as Housing and Urban Development (HUD) undersecretary with his collar on—something that is fairly new, I think.

There are four areas under Baroni's division of HUD. One area is voluntary associations, and Baroni and Patricia Harris, HUD secretary, see that area as the church, because it is a grass-roots organization.

A single pastor or a single congregation may not be able to do a whole lot, but the church in coalition with other churches can bring about some great community building experiences. There are a number of examples. The one I am involved in is a coalition of four churches that have come together to build housing that bridges the gap between two radically diverse communities, the people in Cabrini Green, where the average income was about $3,000 in 1976, and the Gold Coast, where the average income was $54,000.

These churches have been working for nine years, and now that there is a new political administration in the White House, this housing development is possible. If plans continue to function on schedule, this coalition will be able to provide new housing and rehabilitated housing for perhaps one thousand families and to experiment with the first use of solar energy and other methods of energy conservation in urban housing.

This coalition also has members on the local high-school board, which is planning a new plant and curriculum, on the community board that is planning a new park system, and on a neighborhood organization that is working on transportation and streets. Its impact in the community goes beyond this one major project. The church can build successfully, but it needs to do so while political conditions are favorable.

I think the church should be involved in other areas, such as bringing the capital flow back to the dysfunctional neighborhoods. In Chicago, a group of individuals with saintly concerns got together and built a new banking system when the local bank attempted to get its charter moved downtown, because the community had changed to 75 percent black. With the capital flow from this new banking system, whole sections of the South Shore of Chicago are being regenerated. Other service programs might be possible, too. But it is important to look at the needs of the community before a church begins a program and avoid overlap with any other organization or agency.

Finally, I would like to mention three agencies that can help in community self-determination and change. The National Training and Information Center trains groups who are interested in organizing their community. The Center for Neighborhood Technology is attempting to tap federal research and development money for use in urban areas, as well as develop demonstrations of community self-help activities. The Center for Community Change consults with community groups regarding self-help concerns.

Churches ought to also be working with the political entities in the community. We tend to think of political figures as the enemy, but we can't afford to do that anymore. There are ward politicians who need the success of development in their areas and are glad to reinforce community group development.

Last summer thirteen students and I went into the Humboldt Park area to test the viability of housing rehabilitation. But first I went to see the alderman and told him what we were going to do. "Can I come and talk to your group?" he asked. I agreed, but only if he would avoid a political harangue and interact with us, telling us about the needs and resources in his area and how we could be involved in them. And that's what he did, with complete cooperation. In fact he was ready to give us some space in his office. I'm not suggesting that this is always the case, but if that kind of relationship is possible on the West Side of Chicago with its machine politics, it should be possible elsewhere. It's up to the churches to try and to trust God for the outcome.